Galileo

HIS LIFE AND IDEAS

for KIDS

25 ACTIVITIES

RICHARD PANCHYK | FOREWORD BY BUZZ ALDRIN

CHICAGO REVIEW PRESS

LIBRARY OF CONGRESS CATALOGING-IN-PUBLICATION DATA

Panchyk, Richard.
    Galileo for kids : his life and ideas / Richard Panchyk.—1st ed.
        p. cm.
    Includes bibliographical references and index.
    ISBN 1-55652-566-4
    1. Galilei, Galileo, 1564–1642—Juvenile literature.
2. Astronomers—Italy—Biography—Juvenile literature. 3. Physicists—
Italy—Biography—Juvenile literature. I. Title.
    QB36.G2P17 2005
    520'.92—dc22   2004022936

© 2005 by Richard Panchyk
First edition
Published by Chicago Review Press, Incorporated
814 North Franklin Street
Chicago, Illinois 60610
ISBN 1-55652-566-4
Printed in Singapore by CS Graphics
5   4   3   2   1

Cover and interior design: *Monica Baziuk*
Interior illustrations: *Laura A. D'Argo*
Credits: *Front cover (Jupiter), pages vii, 3, 58, 63, and 66; and back cover (rings of Saturn) courtesy of NASA. Pages 24, 43, and 150 courtesy of the National Oceanic and Atmospheric Administration/Department of Commerce. Pages 13, 46, 67, and 118 images © History of Science Collection, University of Oklahoma Libraries. All other illustrations courtesy of Richard Panchyk.*

Two truths cannot be contrary to one another.
—Galileo Galilei, 1613

CONTENTS

✳ 1

SCIENCE AND ASTRONOMY BEFORE GALILEO
I

✳ 2

BEGINNINGS
17

FOREWORD

By Buzz Aldrin

WHEN GALILEO first turned his newly invented telescope toward the heavens, he saw the vastness of the universe. He discovered distant stars, mountains on the moon, and spots on the sun. His work extended our knowledge of astronomy by leaps and bounds. Galileo's belief that the earth revolved around the sun was controversial at the time, but his stubborn insistence on the truth laid the foundation for the modern science of astronomy.

When Neil Armstrong and I set foot on the moon in 1969, it was truly a triumph of science. The revolution started by Galileo had entered a wonderful new phase. Instead of simply gazing into space, we were now traveling there. Instead of looking at moon rocks, we were touching them. I have always believed that space exploration holds great potential. The exploration of space will not only help us understand the science of how the universe works, but it will also help us understand our own planet and ourselves.

Galileo was a genius whose curiosity was his guiding passion. We should all be inspired by his thirst for knowledge. If we strive toward quenching our own thirst for knowledge, we will no doubt send astronauts to Mars and beyond.

Galileo's life story is a wonderful lesson in genius and persistence. Though the events in this book took place 400 years ago, they are still very current.

With every small step we take into space, we should remember that in Galileo's time, just looking into a telescope was a brave step.

Nothing is impossible if we have the courage to turn our dreams into reality and the will to satisfy our never-ending curiosity about the heavens above.

BUZZ ALDRIN, PH.D.
Colonel, U.S. Air Force, Retired
Gemini XII astronaut, 1966
Apollo XI astronaut, 1969

Born in 1930, Buzz Aldrin attended the U.S. Military Academy at West Point. He began his career with the Air Force and flew 62 combat missions in the Korean War. He was selected by the National Aeronautics and Space Administration (NASA) to be an astronaut in 1963. In 1966 he participated in the Gemini XII mission, where he orbited the earth for four days. In 1969 he joined Neil Armstrong and Michael Collins on the Apollo 11 mission to the moon. On July 20, 1969, he became the second man to walk on the moon. Aldrin earned a Ph.D. degree from the Massachusetts Institute of Technology and helped NASA develop methods for space rendezvous and docking of vehicles. He has written several books, including *Return to Earth* (about the Apollo 11 mission) and several science fiction novels.

Buzz Aldrin on the moon, 1969.

AUTHOR'S·NOTE

IN THIS BOOK, I have tried to give readers a broad picture of Galileo's life, discussing his most important scientific discoveries along with the struggles of his personal and public life. My goal was to give readers insight into the man and the world in which he lived.

Throughout the book, I have used the text of letters to and from Galileo. Luckily, much of Galileo's correspondence has been preserved. Some of these have been borrowed from mid- to late 19th century books on Galileo, such as *The Story of Galileo,* Karl von Gebler's *Galileo Galilei and the Roman Curia,* Philarète Chasle's *Galileo Galilei, sa vie, son procès, et ses contemporains,* and Mary Allan-Olney's *Private Life of Galileo.* For some excerpts I have taken the original Italian directly from *Opere di Galileo Galilei* or from Vincenzo Viviani's *Racconto historico della vita di Signor Galileo Galilei, Nobile Fiorentino* and translated them into English. In all cases, the intent is to provide the reader with the best understanding of Galileo's life and times. It is often hard to present in English the forceful yet melodic sense of Galileo's original Italian. Any text in [ ] is an explanation I have supplied about the information given in the quotes.

There are a great deal of scientific and historical terms and personal names mentioned in the book. To help avoid confusion, glossaries of key terms and key people in Galileo's story have been included in the back of the book. There is also a list of key locations, Galileo's key writings, and the popes and grand dukes of Tuscany during Galileo's lifetime. Note that the Jesuits, Dominicans, Benedictines, Carmelites, and Franciscans mentioned throughout the book are all orders of the Catholic Church.

ACKNOWLEDGMENTS

Thanks to all those who have helped and encouraged me during my Galilean odyssey. Very special thanks to the legendary Buzz Aldrin for inspiring me and for writing the foreword. Thanks to Cynthia Sherry for helping me refine the book proposal and see it through the editorial process. Also thanks to my wife, Caren, for her help and encouragement. Thanks to Matthew and Elizabeth for allowing me a few minutes here and there to write this book. And a special thanks to Matthew for helping me test some of the activities. Sincere thanks to all those excellent researchers who have come before me with considerable work to shed some light upon Galileo's life and times.

GALILEO WAS A TRUE GENIUS. Though we think of him mainly as an astronomer, he was a man of many interests. He enjoyed science, mathematics, music, and art and made great discoveries that revolutionized the world. Not simply a scientific philosopher, he also applied his ideas to practical inventions. This is the story of a thinker who was truly ahead of his time.

Galileo sought the truth and argued that there was no substitution for observation and experimentation. He believed that whatever nature was—whatever we observed—must be what God made. Whether or not the Bible or the theologians who studied it said as much, the truth was present all around us, waiting to be discovered. Though his theories contradicted what the Church taught, Galileo was a deeply religious man. He knew the risks of writing that the earth revolves around the sun, but he did not let the threat of punishment stop him. He did not feel that his discoveries should threaten the Church and did not see why religion had to overlap with science.

Galileo's life story is incredibly relevant today. The struggle between science and religion has come up time and again in the years since Galileo lived, not only in Charles Darwin's theory of evolution in the mid-19th century, but also in the moral and religious dilemmas of today. Should we split atoms, alter genes, or clone animals? Do we forge ahead in the name of science, or is there a point at which we should stop?

These key questions of the 21st century also played in Galileo's mind as he made and publicized new discoveries that would change the world. Is knowledge a goal in and of itself? Is knowledge dangerous? As Galileo found out the hard way, science can become very political, because knowledge is power.

The continued exploration of space that Galileo inspired holds the promise to reveal more about our origins. As we discover more, we are sure to run into issues of science versus religion. Perhaps Galileo's thinking was right on target. Perhaps science and religion can remain separate, so long as each maintains respect for the other. As Galileo might have said, both science and religion help us to know ourselves. There is no need to eliminate one for the sake of the other.

TIME·LINE

1054	New star observed by the Chinese
1473	Nicolaus Copernicus born
1543	Copernicus's *Revolution of the Celestial Orbs* published; Copernicus dies
1546	Tycho Brahe born
1564	Galileo Galilei born
1571	Johannes Kepler born
1572	Supernova appears in the sky
1577	Great comet appears in the sky
1579	Galileo studies at a monastery
1581	Galileo begins studies at the University of Pisa
1585	Galileo leaves the university
1589	Galileo begins teaching at Pisa
1591	Galileo's father dies
1592	Galileo forced out of Pisa, accepts position at Padua
1600	Galileo's first child is born
1601	Brahe dies

xii

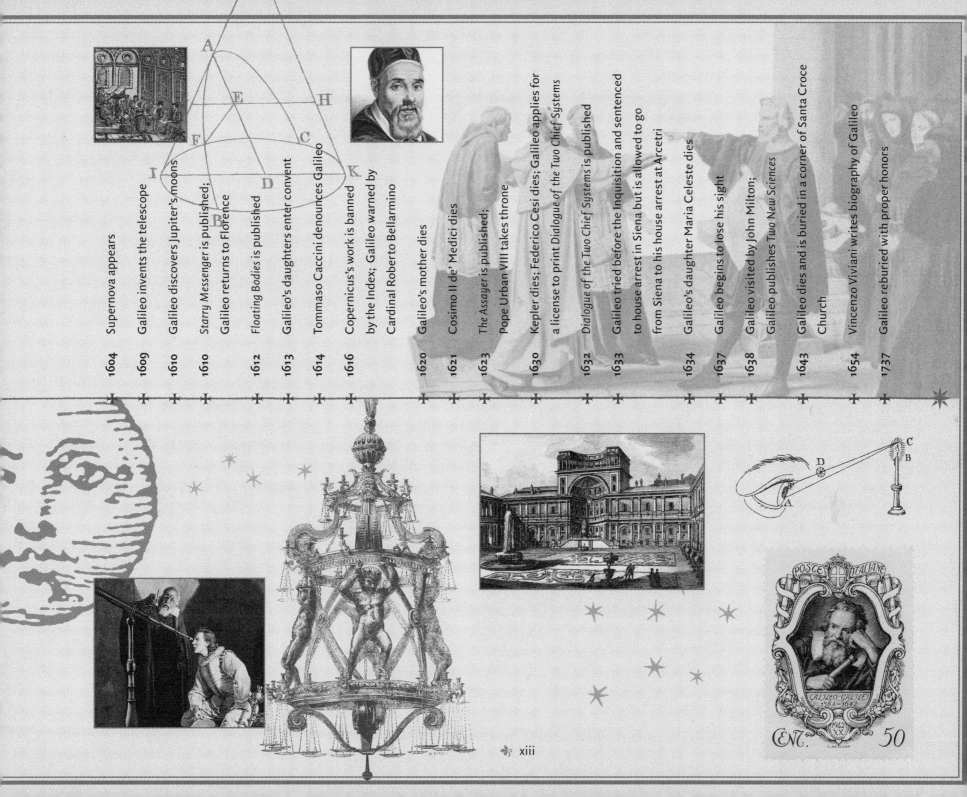

1604	Supernova appears
1609	Galileo invents the telescope
1610	Galileo discovers Jupiter's moons
1610	*Starry Messenger* is published; Galileo returns to Florence
1612	*Floating Bodies* is published
1613	Galileo's daughters enter convent
1614	Tommaso Caccini denounces Galileo
1616	Copernicus's work is banned by the Index; Galileo warned by Cardinal Roberto Bellarmino
1620	Galileo's mother dies
1621	Cosimo II de' Medici dies
1623	*The Assayer* is published; Pope Urban VIII takes throne
1630	Kepler dies; Federico Cesi dies; Galileo applies for a license to print *Dialogue of the Two Chief Systems*
1632	*Dialogue of the Two Chief Systems* is published
1633	Galileo tried before the Inquisition and sentenced to house arrest in Siena but is allowed to go from Siena to his house arrest at Arcetri
1634	Galileo's daughter Maria Celeste dies
1637	Galileo begins to lose his sight
1638	Galileo visited by John Milton; Galileo publishes *Two New Sciences*
1643	Galileo dies and is buried in a corner of Santa Croce Church
1654	Vincenzo Viviani writes biography of Galileo
1737	Galileo reburied with proper honors

xiii

MAP·OF·ITALY

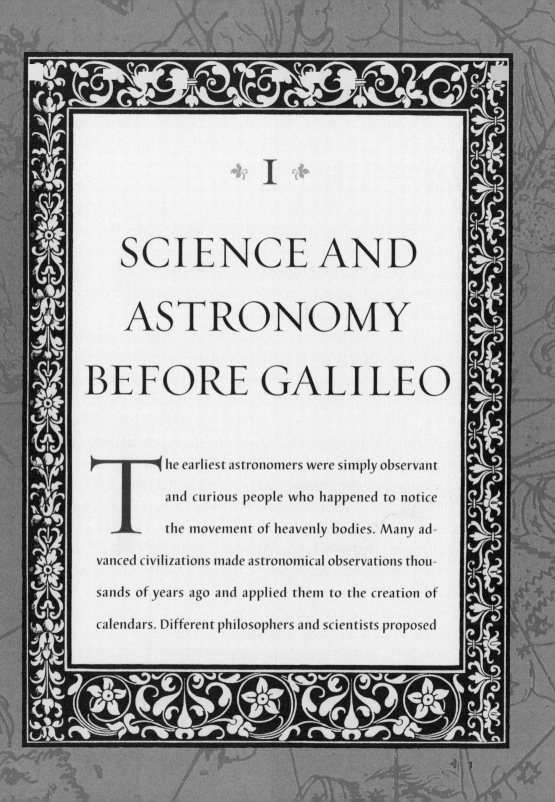

I

SCIENCE AND ASTRONOMY BEFORE GALILEO

The earliest astronomers were simply observant and curious people who happened to notice the movement of heavenly bodies. Many advanced civilizations made astronomical observations thousands of years ago and applied them to the creation of calendars. Different philosophers and scientists proposed

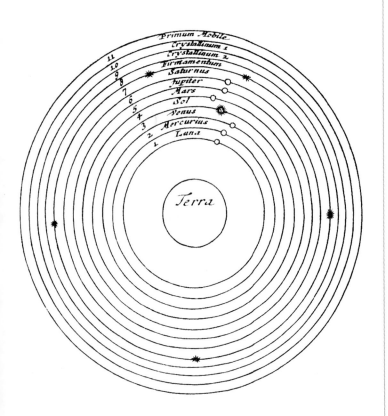

The Ptolemaic system.

various theories over the years. Some thought that the earth was flat. One Greek scientist thought the earth was a cylinder, another that the universe was shaped like an egg. Around 500 B.C. a philosopher and mathematician named Pythagoras (c. 580–c. 500 B.C.) believed that the sun was the center of the world, around which the earth moved.

Aristotle (384–322 B.C.) believed that the earth was round and was at the center of the universe. He believed that the sun and the planets revolved around the earth. Aristotle was the pupil of the philosopher Plato and was himself a philosopher and scientist whose works became the standard in universities across Europe for many hundreds of years after his death. Topics he wrote about included logic, physics (the science that deals with the physical properties of solids, liquids, and gases), and politics.

A great advance in science came around 200 B.C. when Eratosthenes of Cyrene figured out a way to calculate the size of the earth. He used the angle of the sun in the sky at two different places of a known distance apart— Alexandria and Syene (now know as Aswan)—to calculate the circumference of the earth (total distance all the way around the globe). An astronomer named Hipparchus catalogued more than 800 stars that he saw in the sky, and placed them into groups according to their brightness.

The next theory to be proposed was somewhat of a setback for astronomy. Claudius Ptolemy (c. A.D. 100–c. 170) was an Egyptian philosopher and scientist who lived in the great city of Alexandria. He lived at a time when the Romans ruled over Egypt. Ptolemy, the author of an encyclopedia on astronomy, agreed with Aristotle and thought that the unmoving earth was the center of the universe.

In Ptolemy's mind, everything else in the sky revolved around the earth from east to west every 24 hours. The planets and stars were set into hollow spheres around the earth. Each sphere contained different celestial objects: the first sphere closest to the earth contained the moon, the second sphere contained the planet Mercury, the third had Venus, the fourth had the sun, followed by the fifth, sixth, seventh, and eighth spheres for Mars, Jupiter,

Saturn, and the fixed stars, respectively. The theory explained that the sun and moon not only *appeared* to move in the sky, but also in fact *really were moving* around the earth. This scheme of planetary motion became known as the Ptolemaic system.

The ancients saw all the stars in the sky and tried to make sense of what they saw. Mapping and organizing the stars was difficult until people came up with a way to simplify the process. Using the different stars as dots, they connected the points to make the foundation for "pictures" of animals, shapes, and mythological people. The signs of the zodiac are constellations, or groups of stars: Taurus (the Bull), Aries (the Ram), and Leo (the Lion). Other well-known constellations are Orion (the Great Hunter), Cassiopeia (the Queen of Ethiopia), and Ursa Major (the Greater Bear, also known as the Big Dipper).

During the fall of the Roman Empire in the fifth century A.D., barbarian tribes spread across Europe from the east. In Europe, for almost a thousand years, there was a period of limited innovation known as the medieval era, or the Middle Ages. The term "Dark Ages" has also been used but is probably too strong to describe this period. There were of course great artists and scientists during the Middle Ages, but not at the level of earlier times. Elsewhere in the world, however, science still progressed. On July 4 of the year A.D. 1054, Chinese astronomers observed a sudden "new" star in the sky—actually, it was the death of a star, today known as a supernova, or exploding star. The remains of this are known today as the Crab Nebula. This star was so bright it rivaled the moon, and it was even visible during the day for a few weeks.

It was not until about the year 1400 in Europe that creativity and exploration exploded again as it had during ancient Greek and Roman times. The Renaissance (French for "rebirth") that blossomed in 15th-century France, Italy, and Germany was a time for rediscovery of great cultural traditions that had first been introduced thousands of years before. The spirit of the Renaissance was that great minds were open to all subjects. Creativity and

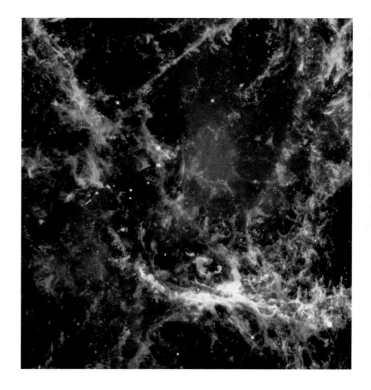

The "new star" of 1054. The arrow points to the core of the star. Clouds of gas expand away from the explosion site to form the Crab Nebula.

invention ruled. Great works of architecture, sculpture, and painting were created during the years 1400 to 1600, using the template of the Greek and Roman masterpieces from 2,000 years before.

EXPLORATION·AND·DISCOVERY DURING·THE·RENAISSANCE

ITALY, AND ESPECIALLY the city of Florence, was one of the most active hotbeds of Renaissance activity, with the likes of the multitalented Michelangelo Buonarroti (1475–1564) and Leonardo da Vinci (1452–1519) working there. Leonardo was an artist and scientist, and he applied his special genius to anything he tried to do. Leonardo's curiosity led to detailed drawings of the various parts of the human body that showed organs and muscles, skin and bones. He was also interested in astronomy and tried to prove mathematically that the sun was larger than the earth.

The rebirth of scientific thought during the Renaissance ran a more bumpy course than did the rebirth of art. Christopher Columbus, Vasco da Gama, Sir Francis Drake, and Amerigo Vespucci were among the many who bravely set sail and explored the world by ship during this period. People still thought the earth was flat until Ferdinand Magellan's crew (Magellan himself had been killed partway through the journey) proved it was not flat by traveling around the globe in the year 1522. Exploration of the world led to discoveries of new continents and the colonization of distant lands.

The science of mapmaking (cartography) slowly blossomed as people realized the true shape of the earth's land masses and bodies of water. Sebastian Münster was a German cartographer who updated the maps of Ptolemy in 1540, and in 1544 published the first edition of his *Cosmography*, a geography of the world enhanced with images of historic events, scientific information, city views from around Europe, as well as the customs and legends of different peoples (see pages 12 and 20 for Münster illustrations). This popular work was reprinted in numerous later editions and translated into several languages. Unfortunately, before he could complete any other works, Münster died of the widespread disease known as the bubonic plague.

(MEN AND WOMEN OF LETTERS)

COMMUNICATION today is easier than ever. Cell phones, beepers, pagers, instant messaging, and e-mail all allow us to stay in touch. Yet all these relatively recent inventions are focused on the quick and the brief. People dash off e-mails in a few seconds and send instant, three-word communications back and forth across an invisible cyberspace.

In Galileo's time, and for more than two centuries after, there was no other means of communication besides writing letters with pen and paper. Letter writing was an art form. Those who were very active in their correspondence were known as men of letters. Lengthy and well-composed letters were commonplace. In fact, many prominent books of the time (including several of Galileo's works) were written in the form of a letter to an acquaintance, scientific or religious colleague, or patron (see sidebar on page 32).

The quill pen needed to be dipped into ink very often, and mistakes were messy. Careful thought was necessary in order to ensure that the words on paper captured the exact phrases and emotions the writer was trying to express. Letters had a structure, with a friendly greeting, introduction, main body, closing, and end greeting.

Many of Galileo's letters to his patrons and friends still exist today, as do the letters his daughter wrote to him from the convent where she lived. In this activity, you will write a letter using a calligraphy pen.

MATERIALS

* Calligraphy pen
* India ink or calligraphy ink (small bottle)
* Paper towels
* Paper

Take the pen and dip it into the bottle of ink. Blot the pen's point on a paper towel before you write. Write on a piece of scrap paper to get the feel for the letters. Notice how the thickness of the lines you draw depends on the angle of the pen tip to the paper. The pens of old could be quite messy, and mistakes were difficult to cover; they simply had to be crossed out.

Try writing a letter such as this:

Most illustrious, enlightened, and devoted friend,

I have received your letter of last month and am most delighted at the prospect of your forthcoming publication. I hope you will send me a copy of your book as soon as it is available. There are several people here to whom I would like to show your work. I think your ideas will find a welcome reception from our community.

Sincere regards from your humble and most reverent friend and servant, (your name)

Gerardus Mercator was another pioneer in map and globe making whose way of depicting the world, known as the Mercator Projection, was a lasting contribution. The Mercator Projection was a method devised for projecting the round globe onto a flat map.

During the Renaissance, more sophisticated navigational instruments helped sailors find their way across the oceans. Still, as late as the mid-1500s, the correct shapes of all the continents and the size of the Atlantic and Pacific oceans were not yet known.

New discoveries were also made in medical sciences: anatomy, biology, and chemistry. Even so, great deadly epidemics of the plague continued to erupt across the cities of Europe during the 1400s and 1500s.

The rebirth of ideas led to a rebirth of literature. All types of writing flourished during this time. Because travel across Europe was slow and difficult (especially across mountainous regions), scientists and great thinkers of the Renaissance communicated through letters. The art of letter writing blossomed, and, in this way, new and revolutionary ideas could be spread to all parts of Europe.

ASTRONOMY·DURING THE·RENAISSANCE

THE RENAISSANCE gave the world beautiful artwork and architecture based on the rebirth of the classical ideas of ancient Greek and Roman times. Unfortunately, astronomy was one place where the theories of classical times should have been abandoned. By 1500 the educated world still believed in the theories of Aristotle and Ptolemy and other ancient scientists and philosophers. During the 16th century, advances in astronomy slowly made headway toward an understanding of the true nature of the universe.

Those scientists who felt it important to make a careful study of the skies included a pair of Polish astronomers, Peter Apian and Nicolaus Copernicus.

PETER·APIAN

PETER APIAN (1495–1552; born Peter Bienewitz) was a noted mapmaker and astronomer who in 1531 made careful observations about the comet (a traveling celestial body made up of ice and rock) later known as Halley's Comet. Apian also observed comets in 1532, 1533, 1538, and 1539. He noted that the tail of a comet seemed always to point away from the sun. In 1536 Apian published a fairly accurate woodcut illustration showing the location of 48 different constellations in the sky. Apian also created astronomical instruments and wrote a book called *Astronomicum Caesareum* (*Astronomy for a King*) in 1540. One of his other contributions was proposing a method of determining lines of longitude (imaginary north-south lines used for navigation) using the distance of the moon to the earth.

NICOLAUS·COPERNICUS

IN 1530 A RESPECTED Polish monk and scientist named Mikolaj Kopernik, more commonly known by his Latin name, Nicolaus Copernicus (1473–1543), finished a book he had been working on for 20 years. It was titled *De Revolutionibus oblure coelestium* (*The Revolution of the Celestial Orbs*), and it completely opposed the Ptolemaic system. Copernicus was a university-educated man who had become a monk. He felt that publishing his book

Nicolaus Copernicus.

would be very risky because of how the Catholic Church might react to the new and strange idea that the earth was not the center of the universe. The Church's teachings said that the earth was the center of creation, and everything else in the universe operated in relation to it. Copernicus also knew that, though they had different opinions than the Catholics on many subjects, the followers of Martin Luther (1483–1546), who broke away from the Catholic Church to form what would become the Lutheran Church, might have the same negative reaction to his new theory.

Copernicus's work proposed that the earth revolves around its own axis (similar to the way a top spins), from west to east, every 24 hours, and that this was the reason the sun, moon, and planets appeared to move in the sky. Copernicus also believed that the sun was the centerpoint around which the earth and other planets revolved.

His friends, including a cardinal and a bishop, practically had to beg Copernicus to get the manuscript published. When he finally did agree to let his book be published in 1543, he tried to protect himself from any possible controversy by dedicating the book to Pope Paul III (1468–1549). By this time, Copernicus was old and very sickly. As he lay on his deathbed, he was brought a copy of the newly printed book.

It was perhaps for the better that the partly paralyzed and senile Copernicus could not see or read it. Editorial changes had been made by his friend Andreas Osiander, who was overseeing the publication of the book. The only problem was that Osiander was a minister, a former Catholic who had converted to the Lutheran faith and who did not believe the Copernican theory should be stated as fact. He had added the word "hypothesis" to the title page. (A hypothesis is defined as merely conjecture—an educated guess—whereas a theory is based more on factual observations.) He also replaced Copernicus's preface with entirely new text, which told readers that astronomy was not necessarily going to provide definitive answers.

Despite these drastic changes, the main body of the work was unchanged. Though seemingly opposed to the views of the Bible that the earth was the

Pope Paul III.

center of the universe and the heavens were unchanging, his work was virtually ignored by the Catholic Church, and none of the popes during the 16th century made any fuss over the book or its theories. Pope Paul III actually liked the book. Martin Luther and some of his followers, however, condemned the book, picking up on the contradictions that the Copernican theory had with some passages of the Bible.

ASTRONOMY·IN·THE·1570s: A·NEW·STAR?

BESIDES COPERNICUS, other Europeans made advances in astronomy during the 16th century. These included Philipp Apian (1531–1589) and Michael Maestlin (1550–1631). Apian, who was Maestlin's teacher at the University of Tübingen, was the son of the mapmaker Peter Apian.

In November 1572 a bright new object suddenly appeared in the constellation Cassiopeia. Astronomers, including Apian and Maestlin, made note of this. Was this object a comet? After all, comets were the only known objects that seemed to appear out of nowhere. But this "comet" was different. It had no tail, for one thing.

Maestlin, a Lutheran, realized that proposing new theories about the heavens could interfere with Lutheran Church ideas. But Maestlin found a way to justify his research of the planets, stars, and comets. He said that by studying the exact nature of these heavenly objects, we would be better able to understand God's design of the universe.

Whatever the truth was about the skies above, Maestlin wrote, it was created by God. In the end it did not matter whether the new truth was different from what we originally thought or not. Whatever we discover to be true, it must be God's truth. Accurate observation was the only path to truth,

(LUNAR OBSERVATION,) PART ONE

SINCE ANCIENT TIMES, people have studied the moon. The varied ways the moon appears in the sky became known as the phases of the moon. Based on the position of the moon relative to the earth, the phases alternate from new moon (where no moon is visible) to crescent moon to half moon to full moon (where the entire moon is visible). In this activity, you will observe the phases of the moon for a two-week period. The key to the scientific progress that took place during the Renaissance was the belief that truth had to be sought through observation. Only through careful study of a topic could the facts be uncovered.

MATERIALS

* Compass
* Pencil
* Notebook of white paper

Set your compass at 2 inches (5 cm) and draw a 4-inch- (10-cm-) wide circle at the center of each of 14 notebook pages. After sunset every day for two weeks, go outside with your pencil and paper. Using the circles you've already drawn as the moon shape, darken the portion that is in shadow. Observe changes in the moon's appearance. How much change is there per day? How long do you think the entire cycle of phases will take?

and was more important than defending old theories. In 1573 he published *Demonstratio astronomica loci stella (Astronomical Explanation about Stars)*. In this work, he wrote that the object that had appeared in the sky was not a comet, and was too far away to be a planet, so it had to be a new star. According to Aristotle's view of the universe, the realm of the stars was supposed to be unchanging. The old teachings said that there was nothing new to be revealed in the skies, no new surprises or secrets. Aristotle believed that whatever was there, it would always be the same. But here was a new star suddenly appearing in the sky! Maestlin wrote in his work that the opinions of Aristotle and Ptolemy were wrong because they contradicted the observations he had made.

TYCHO · BRAHE

ANOTHER PERSON who noted the new star of 1572 was a Danish astronomer named Tycho Brahe (1546–1601). Educated at the University of Copenhagen, Brahe was inspired to take up the study of astronomy by a solar eclipse (an event that occurs when the moon passes in front of the sun) he saw in 1560. An evening duel in December 1566 cost Brahe part of his nose, which he replaced with a gold copy. This did not prevent him from furthering his career, and he designed astronomical instruments including a huge quadrant (an instrument to find the altitude, or height in the sky, of a celestial object) that took many men to construct.

On the night of November 11, 1572, Brahe happened to be studying the sky when he noticed a bright star with which he was unfamiliar. He quickly asked around to see if anyone else had noticed this new star. Brahe made measurements of the location, brightness, and color of the star and followed it over the 16 months that it lit up the night sky. He noticed that the twinkling light grew in intensity over the months of early 1573, until it was brighter than even the star called Sirius and larger than the planet Jupiter. He watched it change from a strong white to yellow to red to blue and then become pale and finally fade away in early 1574. At the urging of a friend, he published his findings in a book.

As we now know, what Brahe and others witnessed was really a supernova. Supernovae are rare events—the last one visible from earth happened in 1604.

BRAHE'S·OBSERVATORY

Tycho Brahe.

INSPIRED BY THE NEW STAR of 1572, Brahe made a comprehensive catalog of 777 stars during the 1570s. In the mid-1570s, Brahe received a generous offer from the king of Denmark, who wanted to ensure that the great astronomer remained in Denmark rather than entertain offers of sponsorship from other kingdoms. His highness granted Brahe an island of his own and promised to fund the construction of a fully equipped observatory, to Brahe's exact specifications. An excited Brahe proceeded to construct several large observatory buildings with towers, at a tremendous cost, sparing no expense to create a showcase of all the available technology. He named the great facility Uraniburg.

In the days before the telescope, observatories relied upon different types of instruments. These could not magnify but were designed to help measure, chart, and describe the objects in the sky. The instruments Brahe ordered (some of which were quite large and heavy) for his observatory included

✛ A sextant (an instrument used for measuring angles) of brass

✛ A half sextant

- ✛ Ptolemy's parallactic rules and Copernicus's parallactic rules (used to determine parallax, or the angular difference in direction of a body as measured from different points)

- ✛ Zodiacal armillaries of brass (instruments with rings showing various components of the heavenly sphere)

- ✛ Equatorial armillaries (instruments with rings showing the equator)

- ✛ Several quadrants

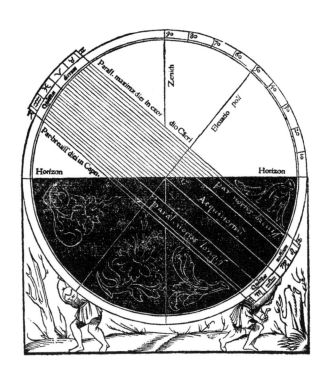

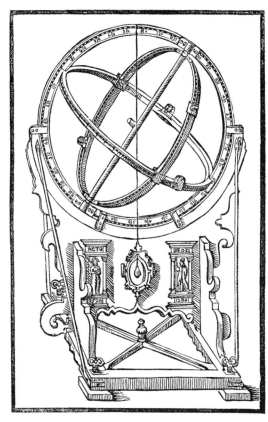

An armillary, from a 1568 edition of Münster's *Cosmography* (above). Pair of astrolabes (right).

- An astronomical ring of brass

- An astrolabe (instrument used to observe the skies)

There, at his custom-built complex, he spent countless nights in observation of the skies. He also taught pupils about astronomy and made many great discoveries during his time in the observatory.

THE·COMET·OF·1577

I N THE FALL AND WINTER of 1577, another spectacular event occurred in the skies. Between November 1577 and January 1578, a great, fiery comet appeared in the skies over Europe. This streak of light with a bright "head" and a long, glowing tail frightened and intrigued people everywhere. Scientists such as Brahe studied the comet closely and made careful notes. Brahe decided that, based on his observations, the comet must be supralunar (meaning above the moon), or exisit even farther away from earth than the moon. The old theories of the ancient Greek philosopher and scientist Aristotle had taught that comets were sublunar (meaning between the earth and the moon). Brahe and others (including Maestlin and Philipp Apian) were certain the comet of 1577 was a distant object, not one planted by God just above the earth.

Once again, this contradicted the views of Aristotle on the nature of the universe. Comets were not simply atmospheric disturbances: they were large objects that moved across the heavens far from the earth. These comets would also appear to move through and across what would be Aristotle's crystalline spheres, something that was not supposed to be possible. Clearly,

Michael Maestlin's book on the comet of 1577.

THE RENAISSANCE was all about the rebirth of knowledge. Gathering and interpreting knowledge was an important way to understand the workings of the natural world. Information was power, and scientists understood this to be true. The artist and scientist Leonardo da Vinci observed very closely the dissection of human bodies to see the details of muscles, bones, and organs. One of Johannes Kepler's professors was a pioneer in weather observation, and he made careful and detailed notes in a journal every day for many years. In this activity, you will do the same.

MATERIALS

✳ Outdoor thermometer
✳ Pencil
✳ Notebook
✳ Graph paper

Place the thermometer outside, in a place where it is not too shady. According to your schedule, choose six or more times during the day when you can check the temperature—for example, 7:00 A.M., 8:00 A.M., 3:00 P.M., 4:00 P.M., 5:00 P.M., and 6:00 P.M. Be sure to get some morning readings and some evening readings. Record the temperature in your notebook every day for two weeks, and use the graph paper and pencil to plot out the daily temperatures.

The power of data is that it can be analyzed to get even more information. That is why data such as this is sometimes called "raw" data. Raw data is very important to scientists because it has the potential to reveal a great deal. That is why Brahe made such careful observations of the sky. So, what can you do with this raw data? There are a few ways to look at the numbers.

What was the average temperature during the two-week period at each of the times of day? To figure this out, add all the temperatures for 7:00 A.M., and then divide by 14 (the number of days you measured). What was the temperature range each day? Take the highest temperature from day one and subtract the lowest temperature from day one. Repeat for all the days. Another way to examine the data is to see what the trend is, if any. Plot the 7:00 A.M. temperatures for each day on graph paper. Draw a line connecting the dots. To examine the trend, as you go forward in time, see if a pattern emerges. The more weeks you measure the temperature at 7:00 A.M., the more likely you are to see an overall trend.

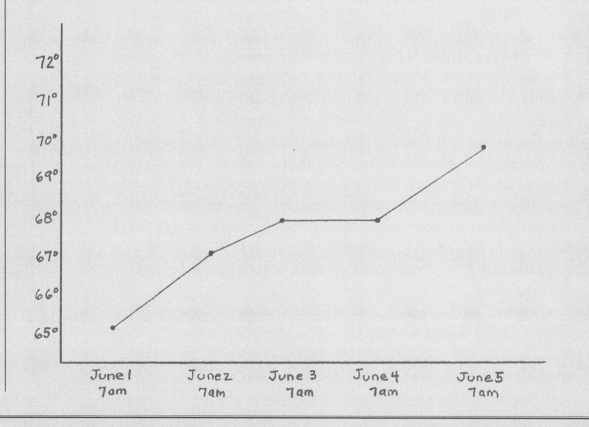

the skies beyond earth's moon were not constant and unchanging, nor were there crystalline spheres that rotated around the earth. As Brahe and others proved, the universe was full of surprises, occurrences that, like comets and supernovae, could not be predicted or fully explained.

Other scholars also studied the comet but came to different conclusions. Jacob Heerbrand, head of religious studies at the University of Tübingen (in Germany), lectured about the comet to his students. He considered it a warning from God directly to the people of the earth, a small taste of divine power. Heerbrand compared God's comet with a father showing his son a switch (a rod or twig used to whip someone) as a sign of what punishment might come if bad behavior continues.

According to Heerbrand and other religious leaders, the comet's appearance was supposed to strike fear in the hearts of men and women because it was a sign from above that sins and evil could not run unchecked in the world. For people who were already uneasy about this bright streak in the night sky, the words they heard in church could only have made them more panicked.

Maestlin went on to teach mathematics and astronomy at the University of Tübingen. Notably, he was one of the first to teach the Copernican theory as an alternative to the Ptolemaic system. One of his students during the 1580s was Johannes Kepler (see sidebar on page 39), a promising young man who went on to become a noted astronomer and a good friend and supporter of Galileo.

Science and astronomy during Galileo's childhood were far from being seen as witchcraft, but they still had a long way to go. The scientists who studied comets and other celestial events were slowly making progress toward understanding how the universe worked. They had to rely upon observation with the naked eye, because they did not yet have any means to magnify the heavens.

It would be up to Galileo Galilei to take the sparks of understanding and ignite them into a blazing fire of discovery.

A 17th-century engraving showing people watching three different comets in the sky.

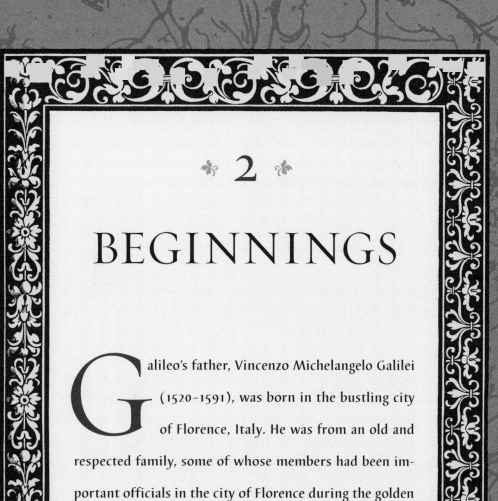

2

BEGINNINGS

Galileo's father, Vincenzo Michelangelo Galilei (1520–1591), was born in the bustling city of Florence, Italy. He was from an old and respected family, some of whose members had been important officials in the city of Florence during the golden years of the Renaissance. His ancestor Tommaso de' Bonajuti was one of Florence's 12 Buonomini (so-called "good men" who were appointed as advisors to the government) in the year 1343. The family had changed their surname

from Bonajuti to Galilei in honor of one of Tommaso de' Bonajuti's sons, whose first name was Galileo. Vincenzo's great-great uncle was Maestro Galileo, a famous doctor and professor of medicine at the University of Florence.

Young Vincenzo was very intelligent and interested in many different subjects. Playing and studying music was his first passion, but he was also a talented mathematician and philosopher. Philosophy was an ancient art, dating back thousands of years to the Greeks and earlier. Philosophers liked to ponder questions about life and think everything through from different viewpoints. For philosophers, debate and logic were subjects that held great interest.

Though it was fun and interesting to have several different interests, Vincenzo was compelled to keep his musical and philosophical pursuits as hobbies. He found that he needed to do business in the wool trade to make ends meet.

In about 1560 Vincenzo Galilei moved from Florence to Pisa, Italy. It was there that he married Giulia Ammannati (1538–1620) on July 5, 1562. The Ammannatis were an ancient and prominent family from the region of Italy known as Pescia (from the Italian word for "fish"). His wife's family was even more important and respected than the Galileis had once been.

YOUNG·GALILEO

GALILEO GALILEI was born on February 15, 1564, in a small room on the second floor of a two-story house in Pisa. He was the first of several children the Galileis would have, among them Elena, Virginia, Livia, and Michelangelo. Galileo's birth came just three days before the death of Michelangelo Buonarroti, the famous Italian painter and sculptor. On

✽ GALILEO'S FAMILY TREE

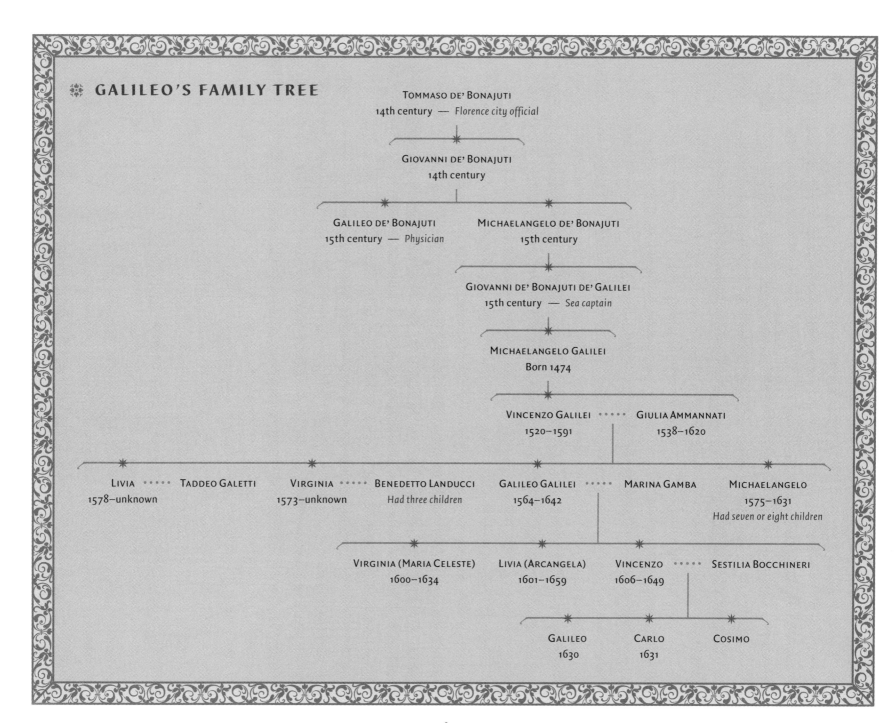

TOMMASO DE' BONAJUTI
14th century — *Florence city official*

GIOVANNI DE' BONAJUTI
14th century

GALILEO DE' BONAJUTI
15th century — *Physician*

MICHAELANGELO DE' BONAJUTI
15th century

GIOVANNI DE' BONAJUTI DE' GALILEI
15th century — *Sea captain*

MICHAELANGELO GALILEI
Born 1474

VINCENZO GALILEI ····· **GIULIA AMMANNATI**
1520–1591   1538–1620

LIVIA ····· **TADDEO GALETTI**
1578–unknown

VIRGINIA ····· **BENEDETTO LANDUCCI**
1573–unknown   *Had three children*

GALILEO GALILEI ····· **MARINA GAMBA**
1564–1642

MICHAELANGELO
1575–1631
Had seven or eight children

VIRGINIA (MARIA CELESTE)
1600–1634

LIVIA (ARCANGELA)
1601–1659

VINCENZO ····· **SESTILIA BOCCHINERI**
1606–1649

GALILEO
1630

CARLO
1631

COSIMO

February 19, 1564, the newborn Galileo was baptized as a Catholic in the beautiful Duomo (cathedral).

In that part of Italy, almost the entire population was Catholic. Martin Luther's Protestant Reformation was an anti-Catholic movement that had begun in Germany 40 years earlier. It did not have much effect on the population in Galileo's area, but it did make the Catholic Church less tolerant of different views.

When Galileo was 10, his father decided the family should move back to Florence from Pisa. By this time, young Galileo showed signs of intelligence, building little instruments and gadgets. These mechanical inventions amused his friends and classmates and impressed his father. Galileo showed signs of curiosity about how things worked. He was very inventive, and if he did not have a part he needed, he improvised and used something else that he had at hand. Like Leonardo da Vinci 100 years earlier, Galileo had a mechanical mind that sought to understand and build machines and inventions.

Though engaged in business, Galileo's father found the time to write and publish several works, including his best known, called *Dialogo della Musica antica e moderna* (*Dialogue of Ancient and Modern Music*). Vincenzo was a creative and very learned man who knew ancient Greek and Roman literature and ancient Greek music. His intelligence drew wealthy and powerful people to him, and he spent time developing relationships with several important people who appreciated his musical theories. When Galileo was about 14, his father was invited to stay with Duke Albrecht of Bavaria, who lived in the German city of Munich, 300 miles (480 km) from Florence.

Vincenzo was also a contributor to the Florentine Camerata, an organization of musicians that experimented with musical drama, leading to the birth of the opera. The Camerata met at the home of a music lover named Count Giovanni de Bardi, who was the leader of the group. Intelligent and important men were among those who belonged to the Camerata and discussed musical theory and experimentation. Among the musical pieces Vincenzo composed was a collection of different musical scales for various instruments.

The Lute Player. Galileo and his father both enjoyed this instrument.

◄ (facing page) City plan of Florence in 1570.

Vincenzo was an expert lute (a stringed instrument similar to a modern-day banjo) player, and he taught young Galileo how to play the little instrument very well. Galileo also learned to play the organ, but the lute remained his passion throughout his life. He also showed great talent and

(COOK A RENAISSANCE MEAL)

GALILEO ENJOYED eating meals in the company of friends and family. He enjoyed fine food and knew a lot about wine. The meals that Renaissance Europeans ate every day were different from what you might eat today. Much of the food we know today was not introduced into Europe until the explorers brought them back from the Americas. The following foods could not be found in Galileo's time: chocolate, coffee, potatoes, squash, and corn (all native to the New World).

Without refrigeration, food had a short life. In the early 17th century, there were no chemical preservatives to keep food fresh. Salt and a variety of spices and herbs were often used to mask the taste of meat that may not have been so fresh anymore. Herbs and spices were also considered to have medicinal benefits.

You can prepare a Renaissance-era meal in honor of Galileo. The menu for this Renaissance meal is meatballs and pea soup.

☽ *Adult supervision required*

INGREDIENTS AND UTENSILS FOR MEATBALLS
Serves 4–6

* Large mixing bowl
* 2 pounds (900 g) ground veal (you could also use beef, turkey, or chicken) or a mixture of meats
* 2–3 slices of crisply cooked bacon, crumbled
* 1 teaspoon (5 ml) coarse salt (sea salt, for example)
* ½ teaspoon (2.5 ml) crushed fennel
* Handful of chopped fresh parsley
* 1 teaspoon (5 ml) dried marjoram
* ½ teaspoon (2.5 ml) dried oregano
* Medium to large frying pan
* 1 teaspoon (5 ml) lard or shortening

Mix all the ingredients together by kneading the meat in a bowl with the bacon, spices, and herbs. Form small balls out of the meat mixture. Heat up a frying pan and put the lard inside. (If a drop of water sizzles on the pan, it is hot enough.) Fry the meatballs on medium heat so that they are brown on all sides. Cut one open to make sure they are done.

INGREDIENTS AND UTENSILS FOR PEA SOUP
Serves 8–10

* 2-quart (4-pt) pot
* 10 cups (2.3 l) water (less if using liquid broth)
* 1 pound (450 g) split peas
* Handful of chopped parsley
* ½ teaspoon (2.5 ml) salt
* Black pepper, to taste
* 2 slices of bacon, crisply cooked, and crushed (optional)
* 3 cubes beef or vegetable broth

Add all ingredients to the pot and bring to a boil. After boiling on high for five minutes, simmer on low, covered, for two hours. Serve and enjoy!

passion for painting and drawing. The Italian Renaissance spawned a great many talented painters, sculptors, and architects, and their works were all over Florence in churches and public places, positioned to inspire future generations. A career in art also appealed very much to young Galileo, and his expertise on the subject later became well known to the painters of the time.

In the meantime, while Galileo was entertaining notions of a career in painting, his father, Vincenzo, was hoping that his son could make a respectable living in the wool trade. But by the time Galileo was in his mid-teens, it was clear to his father that the boy was very intelligent and destined for a different kind of career. Vincenzo realized he would have to give up on the idea of making his son into a merchant. Though a respectable trade was the easy route, Vincenzo felt he had a duty to encourage his son to make use of his intellect. He thought back to his successful ancestors and wondered if Galileo would be the next family star.

One of the things that Galileo learned from his father early on was to examine a problem independently, without taking someone else's word for the solution. According to the writings of Vincenzo, observation was key and led to the path of truth and discovery. Galileo would later apply this lesson to his own work.

Vincenzo was now hopeful that perhaps his young son would study medicine and one day become a doctor. He certainly did not feel that either music or art were the proper career choices for the boy, having seen how difficult it was to live off of music alone.

Galileo spent some time at the Benedictine monastery of Santa Maria di Vallombrosa when he was about 15 years old, learning religion and logic from the monks there. Logic had been a popular topic of study since ancient times. It helped young students understand how to approach a problem, analyze it, and tackle it in a way that makes sense. After a few months, Galileo returned home. The reason his father gave the monks for taking him out of school was "opthalmia," which was an inflammation of the eye membrane.

A 16th-century classroom.

Opusculū repertozii pronosticon in mutationes aeris tam via astrologica q̃ẓ metheozologica vti sapiētes experientia comperientes voluerunt p̃q̃z vtilissime ozdinatū incipit sidere felici z primo pzohemiū.

Om i multis volumi nibus sapientes anti qui de mutationibus aeris multa scripta fecerunt z diuersimode de bac materia tractauerūt: Quidā eni cū alijs a. pposito extraneis comiscendo: Alij vo tractatus speciales plizos tn z obscuros super boc faciēdo: Alij autē tantūmodo recitando nullū tn auctozis a quo dicta sua accepe runt allegando. Quia etiaz qui voluerit aliquid iudicare: durū ē tot libzos inspi cere: totiensq̃ verba obscura fm suum intellectum exponere. Auctozes etiā si videanī discozdes concozdare: aut illa que faciūt ad suū ppositū ab alijs separe: ppter que dicta auctozū specialiter in istis pzibus rema nent in erpta. Ideo cōsiderani p̃bono snias: aut dicta auctozū que fa ciunt ad ppositū nostrū: eosq̃ si discozdes videanī fm pposse cōcozdare atq̃ libzos z capitula quozūverba aut sentētiā recitabo fideliter alle gare: ut si aliquis mibi nō crediderit: aut in ppositionib' in boc reperto rio pōstis addere uel minuere voluerit ad libzos de quibus me iuuare intendo facilius possit recurrere. Utilitas autem operis in boc cōsistit ut videlicet absq̃ pluriū libzozū inspectiōe snias pluriū doctozū facili' z citius possum° ad inuicē compare: z collatione facta ad inuicē ad mi nus illa in quib'magis cōcozdare videbunī tpib'z climatib' nostris p erpientiā certā cōpzobent z appzobent si appzot anda fuerint : uel fm exigentiā erpientie exponantur. Aut si isto tpe aut climate inutilia vī

a 2

Renaissance-era page from a medical text by Hippocrates.

IN 1581, at the age of 17 and a half, Galileo passed his baccalaureate (bachelor's) exam and enrolled at the University of Pisa on November 5. By this point, Galileo was already an excellent artist and musician and knew Greek and Latin. Even though his father knew it would be a strain on the family's finances, Vincenzo nevertheless felt that it was very important to give his son a proper education.

The university in Galileo's time was a place where only the wealthiest and smartest young men went. Girls did not have educational opportunities. For the most part, only future priests and professors went to a university to study. The average boy never dreamed of going there. Most young men in 16th-century Europe grew up to become farmers, servants, or day laborers and could barely write their own names. A few luckier boys were destined to become blacksmiths, carpenters, butchers, or perhaps even merchants. It did not matter if a boy was from the country or the city. A formal education was unnecessary for most professions. Most learning was done through becoming an apprentice to a master (an expert in a particular trade). But Galileo Galilei was lucky. He was smart enough to show promise and fortunate enough to come from a family that was not very poor.

Galileo's first goal upon entering the university was to get his master's degree. On the path to medicine, Galileo was distracted by a geometry lecture he accidentally overheard. Galileo stood fascinated as the beauty and logic of math was laid out before him. It struck a chord deep within him and set his mind afire with new possibilities.

As it happened, the professor whom he had overheard, Ostilio Ricci, was a friend of Galileo's father, and upon hearing of Galileo's interest in math, Ricci allowed Galileo to take the course. At this time in his life, Galileo was not yet very familiar with mathematics. Though his father understood mathematical principles well enough, he did not want to distract his son from his studies in medicine. After all, medicine was a profession in which Galileo could make some decent money. As part of his medical studies, Galileo would have been required to read the works of two ancient Greek doctors, Hippocrates and Galen of Pergamum. Though Galen had been an advocate of experimentation, not much had been done to put his ideas to the test for more than 1,000 years. Unfortunately, medical science had not advanced much since Galen's time, and Galileo was not very interested in it.

But before allowing Galileo into his classroom, Ricci was careful to speak with Vincenzo Galilei in private. Galileo's father reluctantly agreed that he would allow Galileo to study with Ricci. "Do not tell my son I have consented," said the father to the tutor, "lest he think I am agreeing that he should abandon his medical studies." Together, Galileo and Ricci went through the works of the Greek mathematician Euclid. They got to the sixth book when Galileo finally asked his father not to stand in the way of his mathematical pursuits. Vincenzo, seeing how strongly his son really felt about the subject, finally gave up his dream of Galileo becoming a doctor.

AN·INQUISITIVE·MIND

A S HE ATTENDED CLASSES at the university, Galileo was a very eager learner. Learning was something that seemed to come naturally to him from his youngest childhood days. Listening to the professors explain theories on many different topics was fascinating, and it excited Galileo. His father's educated mind had made the atmosphere at home very intellectual. So it was natural that by the time Galileo was of college age, his mind was capable of processing large amounts of mathematical and scientific information and forming opinions on it very quickly.

Bronze lamp in the cathedral at Pisa.

Still, his teachers were becoming a little bit unsettled that their pupil Galileo was never content to simply accept things as they were. The young man with the reddish hair and fire in his eyes had to pick theories apart and try to see if they were really true. He had learned from his father never to accept things as fact just because someone in a position of authority said they were so. It did not matter to him whose facts were being presented. Galileo even questioned the theories of the ancient Greek philosopher and scientist Aristotle. The highly respected Aristotle was required reading in many universities, with the object being for students to learn, understand, respect, and repeat his theories and ideas on physics and other subjects, not to rip them to shreds. This quest for truth would carry Galileo to great dis-

(THE PENDULUM)

NEARLY ALL of the great astronomers made contributions to physics and other sciences. In order to advance their astronomical studies, they had to understand many scientific principles, including gravity and acceleration (increase in speed). Galileo was one of the first scientists to experiment with the properties of the pendulum. He noticed that the period (the amount of time it took for the pendulum to go back and forth once) of a pendulum's swing is related only to the length of the pendulum's rope. The amount of weight attached or the amplitude of swing (how high and far the pendulum swings) does not matter.

Observe for yourself what Galileo first saw more than 400 years ago.

MATERIALS

* Scissors
* Long length (at least 3 feet [1 m]) of thin string (for example, the type used in bakeries)
* 3 weights of different sizes (all of which should be easily attachable to the string)
* Plant hook, flagpole, or other hook that will allow a string with weight to hang unobstructed
* Stopwatch or digital timer that shows seconds

Cut the string into three different lengths (6 inches [15 cm], 12 inches [30 cm], and 18 inches [45 cm]). Attach a weight to one of the strings and hang the string from the hook. Using the stopwatch, time how long it takes for one complete swing (back and forth), pulling the weight to different heights along the arc before releasing it. Now, change weights and time it again. When you have used all the different weights, switch strings and try again using the three different weights. Each string should give you the same period of time, no matter what the weight or amplitude (range) of swing.

coveries in later life, but it would also make him many powerful enemies.

One day in 1583, when he was still only 19 years old, Galileo was in the beautiful Pisa Cathedral after attending a mass. He took notice of the beautifully sculpted bronze lamp that was located in the dome of the cathedral. An attendant had just made an adjustment to the lamp and let go of it. While Galileo watched, the massive lamp was swaying back and forth from the cathedral ceiling like a pendulum. Galileo looked up in fascination. He noticed that no matter how wide the arc of the swing, the time it took for the lamp to swing back and forth seemed to be the same. The first swings were very wide and very fast, he noticed. As the lamp slowed down, its swings became shorter. Since Galileo had no clock to time the swings, he used his pulse to check his theory. He also realized that the reverse was true: the steady swing of a pendulum was an excellent way to measure the human pulse. Based on these first observations, Galileo later invented a machine that helped doctors of his time take people's pulses. It was called a *pulsilogia*.

Galileo was not only observing and experimenting, he was discovering practical applications for his observations. He was moving beyond the philosophical and theoretical discussions of Aristotle and into the realm of applied science, where formulas and theories are applied to real inventions that can improve people's lives and have an impact on the world. The little gadgets he had made as a child

(MAKE A PULSILOGIA)

POCKET WATCHES were unknown in Galileo's time. Galileo's invention, called a *pulsilogia*, helped keep a standard for measuring the pulse, so that a normal pulse could be compared to a racing pulse and a slow pulse.

MATERIALS

* Length of string, about 12 inches (30 cm)
* 6 big-holed buttons or other, similar weighted objects
* 36-inch (90-cm) or less wooden dowel (rod) of a half-inch diameter or less (available at a hardware or craft store)
* 2 friends to help
* Table

Thread the string through each of the weights or buttons. Then, tie a knot at one end of the string to keep the weights or buttons from falling off. Knot the other end of the string, and tie it securely to one end of the dowel. Have a friend hold the dowel flat and steady so that roughly half of it hangs off the edge of the table, and the weighted string hangs suspended in the air. Have the other friend

bring the weight back so that the string is almost parallel to the table's surface. Now, feel your wrist and locate your pulse. When you say "Go!" your friend should release the weight and set the *pulsilogia* swinging.

Have your friends keep track of the number of swings of the *pulsilogia*, while you keep track of the beats of your pulse. When the number of swings reaches 10, your friends should say "Stop!" How many beats of your pulse did you have in those 10 swings?

Now, repeat so that your friends can measure their pulses. Make sure the weight is released at the same point as it was the first time. How do your three different pulses compare?

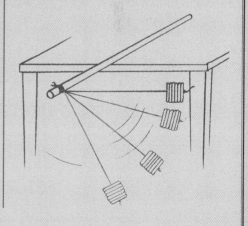

☸ ARCHIMEDES

Archimedes was born in the year 287 B.C. in the time of the ancient Greek Empire. He was a talented inventor and mathematician who lived on the island of Sicily, in the Corinthian colony known as Syracuse. The most famous story about Archimedes goes as follows.

A king sent some gold to a goldsmith with instructions for it to be made into a crown. When he received the finished crown, the king had a sneaking suspicion that it was not actually pure gold. He went to Archimedes for a solution. Archimedes was stumped. Everyone knew that gold was more dense than silver; an equal weight of silver took up more volume (the amount of space something occupies) than gold. However, he thought there was no accurate way to determine the volume of the crown without melting it into a standard shape such as a square, whose dimensions could be measured and volume calculated.

Then, one day, as Archimedes was stepping into a newly drawn bath, the idea hit him. He ran from the bath, crying aloud, "Eureka, I have found it!" The solution was simple. He obtained an ingot, or bar, of gold and an ingot of silver, each exactly the same weight as the crown. He then placed the silver ingot into a vessel of water and carefully marked the level of displacement (how much the water level rose when he added the silver). Next, he placed the gold in the water and marked the level of displacement. Finally, he placed the crown in the water and came up with a level of displacement that lay between the gold and silver. What could this mean? He concluded that since the crown was not as dense as gold, but neither as voluminous as silver, it must be made of a mixture of both gold and silver. The king had his answer. The crown was a fraud.

Archimedes was killed during the storming of Syracuse by the Romans in 212 or 211 B.C. A Roman soldier demanded information while Archimedes was in the middle of trying to solve a mathematical problem. When Archimedes asked not to be disturbed, the Roman soldier killed him. Ironically, Archimedes had designed many inventions to help defend Syracuse against the Roman attack.

Archimedes attempting to solve a problem as a Roman soldier is about to kill him.

helped him gain an understanding of machinery. He was now quite capable of creating sophisticated inventions that went far beyond clever toys.

Though he did well in his studies, Galileo had to leave the university in 1585, before he could complete his doctoral degree. The cost of his son's education was simply more than Vincenzo Galilei could afford. Vincenzo asked the grand duke of Tuscany, Ferdinand I de' Medici (1549–1609), to grant the young genius one of the full scholarships to the school that were reserved for the financially needy. The grand duke decided to turn down the request, based upon the influence of those who were against the young upstart's constant questioning of Aristotelian ideas. Galileo was disappointed, because he enjoyed the intellectual atmosphere of the university.

But that was not the end of Galileo's higher education. In 1586, at the age of 22, after having studied the writings of the ancient Greek scientist Archimedes (see sidebar on page 28), Galileo wrote his first scientific work, in which he told of a new invention. He called his invention *la bilancetta* ("the little balance"). In his piece, he explained how a more effective air/water balance scale (known as a hydrostatic balance) could be created using a counterweight arm that had wire wrapped around it. The number of times the wire was turned around the arm determined how much the counterweight had to be adjusted when used in water.

Besides density (also know as specific gravity), Galileo also was interested in several other subjects explored many years before by Archimedes. The Greek mathematician invented a pump called the Archimedes Screw that could lift water from a river for irrigation purposes; Galileo designed a horse-powered pump to irrigate crops. Archimedes also invented several types of military contraptions including catapults and other weaponry; Galileo studied the motion of projectiles (objects thrown or propelled through the air) and the design of military fortifications.

(SPECIFIC GRAVITY)

GALILEO HAD BEEN interested in the properties of water and the effect solids had on it since his early days in Pisa. He invented a hydrostatic balance that could weigh objects in and out of water. The use of water in weighing objects dated all the way back to the legendary tale of Archimedes. The displacement of water by an object can determine its specific gravity, or density. Different objects of the same weight and different sizes or volumes will displace different amounts of water. In this activity, you will demonstrate this principle.

MATERIALS
* Tub or washbasin
* Water
* Brick (can find in a garden or home supply store)
* Masking tape
* 1-quart (2-pt) plastic container or large plastic tumbler

Fill the tub halfway with water. (Note: the water line should be lower than the height of your cup or plastic container.) Place the brick into the water so the brick is standing on end. Record the new level to which the water has risen by placing a piece of masking tape there. (Use the bottom of the tape to mark the line the water has risen to.) Now, remove the brick. Take the empty cup or container, and place it into the water standing right side up (no water should get inside the cup). Observe the water level. How much water does this very light object displace compared to the very heavy brick?

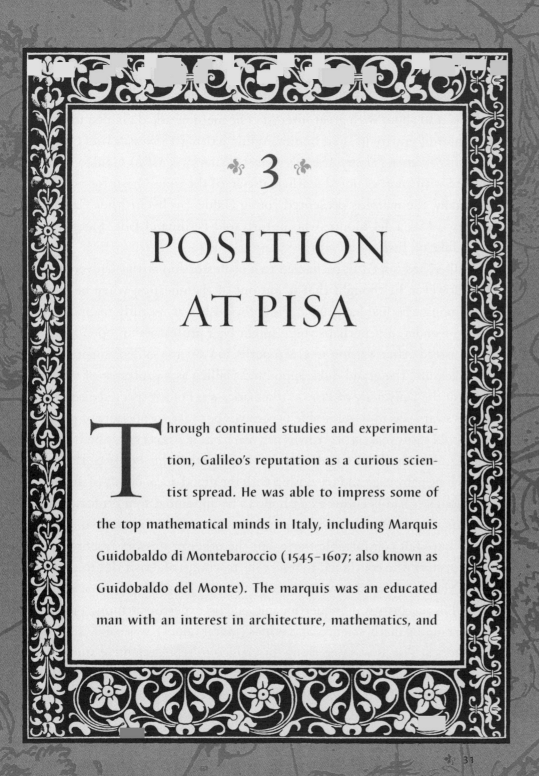

❧ 3 ❧

POSITION
AT PISA

hrough continued studies and experimentation, Galileo's reputation as a curious scientist spread. He was able to impress some of
the top mathematical minds in Italy, including Marquis
Guidobaldo di Montebaroccio (1545–1607; also known as
Guidobaldo del Monte). The marquis was an educated
man with an interest in architecture, mathematics, and

astronomy. He began to correspond with Galileo (only in his early twenties at this point), whose earliest mathematical and scientific experiments the marquis read about with great interest. The marquis asked Galileo to study the center of gravity in solid bodies. While writing *Theoremata circa Centrum Gravitatis Solidarum (Theory About the Center of Gravity in Solids)* Galileo corresponded with another noted mathematician of the time, Cristoforo Clavio. Eventually, the marquis presented young Galileo to his brother Cardinal Francesco Maria del Monte, who in turn told Ferdinand I de' Medici, the grand duke of Tuscany, about the young scientist.

Galileo had hoped to be named to a professorship at the University of Pisa. However, he thought that it was out of the question when he heard that a monk who had lectured at Pisa previously was recently reappointed. Galileo wondered if perhaps there might be a professorship open at Florence instead. After waiting several months, in 1589, to Galileo's surprise and great pleasure, the grand duke appointed Galileo as a professor of mathematics at the University of Pisa. Mathematics was not a respected discipline, and his salary was to be a humble 60 crowns per year (professors of philosophy could easily make 400 crowns per year), but it was certainly better than nothing. What he did not realize at the time was that this would be the start of a lifelong patronage and friendship with the grand ducal family of Tuscany.

Though it had been his exact hope to be appointed to a professorship, Galileo's time at Pisa was not so pleasant. Pisa was his hometown and he should have felt comfortable there, but the other professors resented this young upstart who continued to reject the teachings of Aristotle. To professors of the day, Aristotle's widely used texts were the Bible of the academic world. His authority was unquestionable, and his expertise on numerous subjects, including math, science, and ethics (moral values), was solid. To these professors at Pisa, it was one thing for Galileo to rebel as a mere student at the university, but another matter entirely for him to spread his ideas to hundreds of his own impressionable students. His only friend and ally at Pisa was the chair of the philosophy department, a man named Jacopo Mazzoni.

As a philosopher, he was more open to Galileo's ideas and did not think harshly of him. In fact, Mazzoni stayed in touch with Galileo for many years.

One of Galileo's ideas that went against Aristotelian theory dealt with the very mechanics of physics. Aristotle's writings taught that the heavier of two falling bodies released from the same point would reach the ground first. He had written that each object would travel at a speed in proportion to its weight. On the surface, this proposition seemed logical. Of course a small object made of lead would travel more slowly than a large object made of lead. The large object is more massive, so it would go faster. The proposition made enough sense that no one had challenged it for more than 1,000 years.

Once again, Galileo was not one to accept things as fact just because they were written on paper. As he had learned as a child building his own little gadgets, experimenting was the only way to know the absolute truth about anything. The only way to prove Aristotle wrong was to recreate the experiment and put the theory to the test, which, as far as he knew, had never been done before.

Legend has it that one day Galileo climbed to the top of the famous local landmark, the leaning Tower of Pisa. (The tower, begun during the 1100s and completed in 1350, leaned several degrees to one side due to the inability of the soft, sandy soil to support the heavy weight of the building.) There he proved publicly that falling bodies of different weights will accelerate at the same speed.

As the objects Galileo dropped hit the ground below, their simultaneous thuds seemed to show that Galileo was right. Yet some of the students and professors and other onlookers who watched the experiment did not necessarily believe that Aristotle had been proved wrong, only that Galileo was a troublemaker.

"His experiments prove nothing," the nonbelievers said. "Aristotle cannot be wrong."

"How dare Galileo stand against what is commonly held as the truth?" they all gossiped.

The Leaning Tower of Pisa.

NICOLAUS COPERNICUS, Galileo, and many astronomers after them were very interested in how the force of gravity acts on objects, both on earth and in space. Galileo's fabled work while living in the Italian city of Pisa proved that gravity exerted an equal force on objects of different sizes and weights. An understanding of gravity was critical for astronomers to discover the laws of the universe and planetary motion. In this experiment, you will attempt to observe Galileo's idea.

MATERIALS

* Orange
* Dime
* Sheet of paper

Stand with the orange in one hand and the dime in the other. Hold your arms straight out in front of you, perpendicular to your body. Drop the orange and coin at the same moment. Observe that they both hit the ground at the same time. Size or weight did not make a difference in the gravitational pull on the objects.

Now, try the same thing with the orange and the sheet of paper. Which hit the ground first? Why did gravity act dif-

ferently this time? The answer is that gravity did not act differently, but something interfered with gravity's ability to pull the paper to the ground. The paper's shape and its light weight allowed it to "float" momentarily. Crumple the paper into a ball and try it again. What happens?

Because the earth has an atmosphere made of several gases (what we call "air"), objects such as gliders, parachutes, and feathers can seemingly defy the laws of gravity by taking advantage of the properties of the gases that make up air. The paper acts lighter than the air and is buoyed by the air for that moment it floats around before hitting the ground. On a planet with no atmosphere (no gases or air), that sheet of paper would reach the ground at the same time as the orange.

This experience showed Galileo that some people were very stubborn, and it did not matter if the truth stared them in the face. These people would always deny what they saw no matter what. Galileo would encounter such nonbelievers for the rest of his career.

MAKING·ENEMIES

IN THE EYES of his old-fashioned colleagues, Galileo was heading down a path of no return. The other professors at Pisa had trouble coexisting with this bold and opinionated man who was turning their world upside down. Then, something happened that changed Galileo's future at Pisa. An ambitious local nobleman and architect named Don Giovanni de' Medici had invented a machine that he submitted to Galileo for his opinion. Medici was a member of an ancient and powerful Italian family. The purpose of his invention was to dredge the harbor of the city of Livorno (Leghorn) and clean it by removing the mucky bottom. This would help make the harbor safer for ships to dock.

After studying the contraption, it was quite clear to the brilliant young scientist that it was not well designed and would not work when put to the test. Galileo was not sure what he should do. He thought that perhaps he ought to be delicate and pretend to be impressed with the machine. Uncertain, he carefully pondered his options. Though the noble inventor was from a very powerful family, Galileo decided to be honest. The truth must be known, he thought, and he criticized the machine in public. Perhaps he was too forceful in his criticism; perhaps it bordered on mockery. In any event, Giovanni de' Medici was not at all pleased by the tone of Galileo's remarks.

Then, when Giovanni went to try the machine out, its failure proved that Galileo had been correct. This enraged the nobleman further, to the point of action. His reaction was swift and decisive. He vowed to remove Galileo from Tuscany (the region where Pisa is located). Galileo's friend Marquis Guidobaldo del Monte sensed that the situation was rapidly becoming explosive and advised his friend to resign his position at the University of Pisa—much to the delight of the other professors.

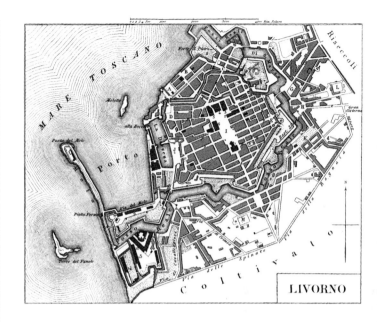

The port of Livorno.

A·NEW·POSITION

BUT THERE WAS HOPE yet for Galileo. With the help of his defender the Marquis Guidobaldo, who called him the "Archimedes of his time," he was able to obtain a position as chair of mathematics at the University of Padua. The position had been left unfilled after the death of its previous holder, a man named Moleti. Galileo applied and was found fit to fill the role. He was very grateful to Guidobaldo for his help. In fact, years later, when the marquis died, his son wrote to Galileo and told him he had been loved by the marquis, and he hoped that Galileo could therefore share in the family's sorrow at losing him.

Galileo soon relocated to the town of Padua, located about 130 miles (210 km) northeast of Pisa, near the city of Venice. It was not that far from Pisa in actual distance, but in the attitude of the community it was a million miles away. When he first arrived at Padua, he found a most gracious reception in the home of a noble scholar named Vincenzo Pinelli, who was said to have more than 75,000 books in his massive library.

Galileo gave his first lecture at Padua in December 1592, with a new salary of 180 florins (more than he had been making before). The biggest advantage of this position was that Galileo was now free to pursue his science without fear of being attacked and ridiculed by his fellow professors. He was a popular professor with crowded classrooms as well as students whom he tutored in private. Teaching was a natural way for this very enthusiastic and opinionated man to get satisfaction that his ideas were being spread.

In addition to teaching classes in geometry and astronomy, Galileo had the time and desire at Padua to experiment, invent, and write. His interests were wide ranging, and he continued to be fascinated with understanding how mechanical things worked and with improving their performance. In 1593 he wrote a treatise on military fortifications and mechanics. He was invited to Venice to evaluate where a rowing ship's oars should be positioned to allow for the maximum efficiency. In 1594 he patented a pump, powered by the movement of one horse, that could be used for raising water to irrigate crops easily.

Some of his inventions were in demand in various locations in Italy and other lands, and Galileo simply could not devote the necessary time to make the instruments himself. In July 1599 he hired a talented workman named Marcantonio Mazzoleni, who oversaw the standardized production of instruments Galileo invented, such as the sector. The sector was a very popular instrument that was used to measure angles, and it had different mathematical scales inscribed on it. One use for the sector was to determine the exact angle of a cannon's aim.

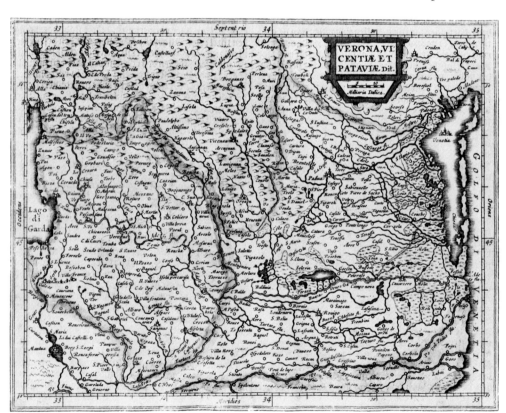

Map showing Venice and Padua (upper right), early 17th century.

36 ❧

Galileo found it necessary to publish an instruction book, or user's manual, for this sector, called *Operazioni del Compasso geometrico e militare* (*The Operation of the Geometric and Military Compass*). More than 200 of these instruments were made under Galileo's direction. He explained and lectured on his inventions to German and Austrian princes and counts, including Philip, Landgrave of Hesse (Germany).

❧ GALILEO AND DANTE

Galileo was interested in art and literature as well as science. During his time at Pisa, he gave lectures on the work of another well-known Florentine named Dante Alighieri. Born in 1265 to an old Florentine family, Dante was a writer who was also involved in the politics of his city. He was later banished from Florence due to his involvement in a political party that had criticized the pope, and he died in Ravenna, Italy, in 1321. He is considered Italy's greatest poet, due to the accomplishment of his great epic poem, *La divina commedia (The Divine Comedy)*, written between 1308 and 1320.

The Divine Comedy is an epic poem divided into three parts, *Inferno* ("hell"), *Purgatorio* ("purgatory"), and *Paradiso* ("paradise," or "heaven"). The three divisions represent the Divine Trinity of God: Father, Son, and Holy Spirit. The long poem is divided into 100 (considered a perfect number) cantos, or sections, 33 in each of the three parts plus a prologue, or introductory section. In fact, the whole poem deals with demonstrating the order of the universe. All three parts of the poem end in the word "stars," representing all that is good beyond this earthly home, perfect order, and the work of God.

In his lecture, Galileo tried to plot out the location and dimensions of hell based on the writings of Dante. In the book, hell is divided into nine concentric circles in three groups, and is a funnel-shaped opening to the center of the earth, the farthest point from God. Punishment is doled out appropriately according to the sin, from least to greatest of evils. In Dante's grand scheme, the punishment always fits the crime in degree and design. Sins of weakness of the flesh come before those of weakness of the spirit, with the greatest of sins sinking deeper into hell.

Heaven is described as ascending circles of the celestial universe. The seven planets—in the order moon, Mercury, Venus, sun, Mars, Jupiter, and Saturn—are followed by the constellations (fixed stars), and then *primum mobile*, the *outermost* circle that moves all the others. This totals nine circles (much like the Ptolemaic system).

Dante Alighieri.

THOUGH GALILEO was already a brilliant mathematician and scientist, by the mid-1590s he had yet to make any major contributions to the field of astronomy. At this point, Galileo still believed in the Ptolemaic system of planetary motion, which said that the sun and the other planets revolve around the earth. One day a foreign scientist came to Italy and lectured on the Copernican theory, which said that the earth and other planets revolve around the sun. Galileo avoided the lectures, thinking them to be nonsense. But being of an endlessly curious nature, he did afterward venture to speak with some people who had attended the lecture. Many people said they were amused by the ridiculous theories, but one attendee would not rule out the possibility that Copernicus just might have been right.

At that moment, something dawned upon Galileo. He realized that all converts to the Copernican theory had once believed in the Ptolemaic system, but that none of Ptolemy's followers had converted from believing in the Copernican theory.

To sum up his feelings on the subject, Galileo wrote: "I began to believe that, if anyone who rejects an opinion that has been embraced by an infinite number, shall take up an opinion held by only a few, condemned by all the schools . . . it cannot be doubted that he must have been induced, not to say driven, to embrace it by the most cogent [convincing] arguments."

Galileo was intrigued by the idea that the sun, not the earth, was at the center of the known universe. Even after he began to doubt the ancient ideas about planetary motion, he still taught the Ptolemaic system to his classes. The timing did not yet seem right for him to openly embrace this explosive new theory. As his sharp scientific mind tackled the problem in depth, by 1595 Galileo finally had no doubt that Copernicus was correct.

❁ THEORIES OF PLANETARY MOTION

Aristotle and Ptolemy proposed theories that said the earth was at the center of the universe, and the sun and planets revolved around it.

Copernicus, Tycho Brahe, and René Descartes proposed systems that said the earth and the other planets revolved around the sun.

In 1597 the German astronomer and scientist Johannes Kepler (see sidebar below) had been out of the University of Tübingen for three years. The 26-year-old Kepler sent Galileo a gift, having heard good things about the Italian genius. The present was a copy of Kepler's book, called *Prodromus*

❈ JOHANNES KEPLER

Johannes Kepler (1571–1630) was Galileo's contemporary, and, like Galileo, he was a multitalented genius who made contributions to various fields in both math and science. Kepler and Galileo were friendly and shared their discoveries with each other.

Kepler was born in the town of Weil der Stadt, Germany. He had a difficult childhood, suffering from smallpox and being taken out of school and put to work when his father had to pay off a friend's debt. When he was able to return to school, he was bright enough to pass the exam for the special schools. He took advantage of a scholarship system that allowed smart young boys a free education if they promised to use it to become pastors or teachers and go where they were needed. Kepler entered the local monastery school, where he lived a strict religious life and studied Latin and Greek. He then passed his bachelor's exam, and on September 15, 1588, he was accepted into the prestigious University of Tübingen.

There, even though his program of study stressed religion, Kepler was able to benefit from a tradition of scientific observation. His astronomy and mathematics professor, the great Michael Maestlin, was his mentor and instilled in him a love of astronomy. (Maestlin's teacher had been Philip Apian, who had also closely observed the night skies and taken notes about his findings.)

While at Tübingen, Kepler was taught the Copernican theory, something that was not yet being taught in Italy. An eager student, Kepler devoured the various subjects he was required to study, including geometry, physics, ethics, writing, debating, Greek, and Latin. He took his master's degree in 1591 and continued on with advanced studies at Tübingen for a few years more.

While most of the others in his program went on to become pastors, Kepler was too drawn by a love of mathematics to be a pastor and instead went into science. After he left Tübingen in 1594, he became a mathematics and astronomy teacher in Graz, Austria. He began to study the orbits (the paths around the sun) of the planets in 1595 and published his findings.

He went on to make important discoveries in the field of astronomy, physics, and optics (the study of lenses and the eye), and also began to correspond with Galileo (who was seven years older than Kepler) as word of the Tuscan genius spread through the scientific community in Europe.

Johannes Kepler.

SCIENTISTS such as Galileo did not hesitate in their search for the truth about the way the universe works. It did not matter if they had to call into question old theories (Aristotle) or even parts of new theories (Copernicus). Though he believed in the Copernican theory, Galileo's friend Kepler proved Copernicus wrong in one regard. Planets do not orbit the sun in perfect circles, but rather in slightly flattened-out circles called ellipses. Kepler sought to explain the way planets revolved around the sun, so he looked to the ellipse for a mathematical and scientific explanation of the laws the planets observed.

A circle has one central point. A planet whose orbit was a perfect circle would orbit around the central point. An ellipse has two central points called foci. An ellipse that is almost a perfect circle has two focal points that are very close together. The flatter (or more stretched out) the ellipse, the farther apart the focal points are from each other.

Kepler's first planetary law is that the distance (A) from the first focal point to any point along the ellipse plus the distance (B) from the second focal point to the same point along the ellipse will add up to the same number. The formula is

A + B = constant

MATERIALS
* Thin string (about 8 inches [20 cm])
* 2 pins with colored heads
* Corkboard (bulletin board)
* Sheet of 8 ½-by-11-inch (20-by-30 cm) white paper
* Pencil (sharpened)
* Color marker
* Ruler

Tie one end of the string to a pin, and the other end to the other pin. Place the white paper on the corkboard so that the long side of the paper is on top, and the board is flat on a flat surface. Now, stick one pin into the paper and corkboard about 1 inch (2.5 cm) left of the center of the paper. Place the other pin about 1 inch (2.5 cm) to the right of the center of the paper.

Take the pencil point under the string and move the pencil toward the top of the paper until the string is taut (tightly drawn). Now, begin to draw a line to the right, keeping the string taut as you go. If you keep the string taut and let the pencil guide you, you will see an arc-shaped line develop. Work back to the middle and then go left.

Replace the pencil tip so it is above the string and move the pencil toward the bottom of the paper until the string is taut again. Draw the rest of the ellipse by following the taut string as far as it takes the pencil in both directions.

Remove the pins and draw dots with the colored markers where the pins were. These are the foci of the ellipse. Pick any two points along the ellipse and stick your pins there. Measure the distance from each focal point to pin 1 and then from each focal point to pin 2. Does A + B = the same? It should, because you already demonstrated the principle with the string. After all, you used string of a fixed length that was attached to each focal point, and you drew the ellipse. As you drew the ellipse, the distances from the foci to the line you drew changed, but the total length of the string remained the same.

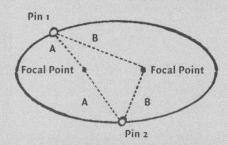

Dissertationum Cosmographicum. Published in 1596, its full name translated into English was *Prodromus of Cosmographical Dissertations; containing the cosmographical mystery respecting the admirable proportion of the celestial orbits, and the genuine and real causes of the number, magnitude, and periods of the planets, demonstrated by the five regular geometrical solids.* The book contained Kepler's careful investigations of the shape and timing of planetary orbits.

Galileo was quite pleased with this fine book, and perhaps was even more pleased with the gesture of friendship that it implied. In his thank-you letter to Kepler in August 1597, Galileo complained that truth seekers were few and far between in the world: "I consider myself happy, in the search for truth, to have such a great ally as yourself . . . It is quite pitiful that there are so few people who seek truth . . . this is not the place to mourn over the miseries of our times, but to congratulate you on your excellent discoveries in confirmation of truth."

He confessed to Kepler that he had some years before adopted the ideas of Copernicus and had collected many arguments against the Ptolemaic system, but had been afraid to publish his ideas because of their controversial nature: "I have so far not dared to publish these ideas, for fear of meeting the same fate as our master Copernicus, who, although he has earned undying fame with a few people, amongst very many people he seems only worthy of ridicule and derision, so great is the number of fools."

Galileo told his new friend that he would consider publishing his ideas if only there were more people like Kepler in the world. Kepler replied in his next letter, dated October 1597, that Galileo could always publish in Germany, where there would be less of an uproar. Though the Protestants were against the Copernican theory, their power was not nearly as strong as that of the Catholic Church. In Germany, royalty ruled the various territories, and the Protestant Church did not have the authority to punish. On the other hand, among Catholics, the pope represented a supreme authority that rivaled that of any royalty. The Catholic Church could arrest anyone whom it felt had spoken against its authority.

For example, in the late 16th century, an Italian philosopher named Giordano Bruno believed the universe was infinite and had other solar systems besides the one where the earth resided, each with planets revolving around their suns. He had also published a work called *Cena de le Ceneri* (*The Ash Wednesday Supper*) in 1584 in which he defended the Copernican theory. He lived in England, France, and Germany before being arrested by the Inquisition (see sidebar on page 91) in Venice in 1591. It seemed the Inquisition was more interested in Bruno's theological (relating to religious study) mistakes about Christ (whom he called a magician rather than a God) than in his Copernican beliefs. Bruno was imprisoned for several years. When he refused to recant (take back) his views, he was labeled as a heretic, or someone who speaks against the Church, and was burned at the stake in Rome in

(LODESTONE EXPERIMENT)

DURING THE LATE 1500s and early 1600s, Galileo became fascinated with magnets. The magnets at the time were naturally occurring iron-laden rocks called lodestones. Galileo went through some trouble to obtain a 56-ounce (1.5-kg) lodestone to give as a gift to one of his most important patrons, Cosimo II de' Medici. The magnet, a symbol of strength, could lift more than its weight in iron. Understanding how magnets worked and what their properties were was a natural curiosity for any scientist of the time. Now, hundreds of years later, we see how magnetic fields are important parts of complicated machinery.

In this activity, you will determine how much a magnet of a given size can lift.

MATERIALS
* 3 or more magnets, different sizes (from a hobby or science store)
* Small, accurate scale
* Pencil
* Notebook
* 2 boxes of small paper clips

Weigh each magnet on the scale. Write down their weights. Take the smallest magnet and see how many paper clips it will pick up. When the maximum number of clips has been lifted, remove them and weigh them. Try this with the other magnets. How much can a magnet carry in relation to its own weight? Express this as a percentage. Divide the weight of the clips into the weight of the magnet and multiply by 100 to get the number.

the year 1600. Though Kepler's suggestion about publication abroad was tempting, Galileo did not publish anything at that time, and he continued to teach the old planetary system until about 1600.

Meanwhile, Kepler had also sent a copy of his book to the famous astronomer Tycho Brahe, who was very impressed with the young genius. A few years later, in 1600, Kepler visited Brahe for a few months and studied Mars's orbit. Soon after, the 55-year-old Brahe hired Kepler to be his official assistant at his observatory near Prague (in what is now the Czech Republic). Upon Brahe's death in October 1601, Kepler was named as his successor to the title of imperial mathematician and was the heir to all of Brahe's research. One of Kepler's projects was to complete the work he had begun with Brahe, the *Rudolphine Tables* (in honor of the emperor), which were finally published years later. The finished book contained a catalog of stars; tables of data about the planets, sun, and moon; and mathematical formulas for use in astronomy.

Title page from Johannes Kepler's and Tycho Brahe's *Rudolphine Tables*, 1627.

SICKNESS·AND·MONEY·TROUBLES

DURING GALILEO'S time at Pisa, his elderly father Vincenzo died on July 2, 1591. As the oldest son, tradition said that Galileo would be responsible for providing for the rest of his family and making sure they lived in relative comfort, without any needs left untended. This included Galileo's unmarried sisters. His sister Virginia had married before their father died, but it still fell on Galileo to pay off the dowry, the traditional gift of money that the bride's family gave to the groom's family upon a wedding. At the time, Galileo did not have enough money to pay his brother-in-law. It was no laughing matter. In 1593 Galileo's mother wrote him a letter asking him to come home and visit, and to please bring money for the brother-in-law, Benedetto Landucci. Though the wedding had been years earlier,

(LUNAR OBSERVATION, PART TWO)

OBSERVATION is good because it can help you understand something for yourself. As Galileo and others before him discovered, observation is the key to learning. It is also a useful exercise in training the eye to notice things. In this activity, you will continue your studies of the moon.

MATERIALS
* Compass
* Pencil
* Sheet of 8 ½-by-11-inch (20-by-30-cm) yellow construction paper
* Scissors

* Sheet of 11-by-17-inch (30-by-45-cm) white paper
* Glue stick
* Watch

Using your compass, draw eight 1-inch- (2.5-cm-) diameter circles on the sheet of yellow paper. Cut out the circles. In the early evening on a clear day, just after sunset, go outside and locate the moon. Facing the moon, note the various structures and trees that are in front of you and on either side of you. On the white paper, draw the trees, houses, streetlamps, or other landscape you see below the moon. Use the glue stick to paste one of the colored circles onto the paper in the position where it appears. Write the time inside the circle. Go back outside a half hour later and find the moon again. Paste another colored circle where the moon's new position is and write the time on it. Repeat this again every half hour for as long as you are allowed to stay up.

Landucci had not forgiven Galileo his obligation. In fact, he was getting very tired of waiting for the dowry and now threatened to have Galileo arrested for failing to live up to his duties.

In 1593 Galileo also first developed a sickness that would bother him for the rest of his life. He had fallen asleep in front of a cold draft of air and, after he awoke, became sick with a variety of symptoms, including pain, sleeplessness, and loss of appetite. He took every new symptom seriously, and for the rest of his life often complained of not feeling well. Though he had some real illnesses, he also could be considered a hypochondriac—someone who gets very worried about every cough, sneeze, and pain.

FAMILY·COMPLICATIONS

AFTER SOME NEGOTIATIONS, Galileo's younger brother, Michelangelo, was set up to go to the distant land of Poland and serve in the court of a nobleman there. Those noblemen who could afford it had a variety of employees in their court who lived there and provided entertainment or philosophical discussions for the noble family. These noblemen served as patrons who provided money for scientific research, artwork, and other projects.

Galileo wanted to get Michelangelo a position closer to home, but there were no such openings. After a tense period of waiting, the Polish prince finally agreed to take Michelangelo Galilei. As part of the deal, Michelangelo would have two servants and a good salary of 300 crowns. Galileo thought it would certainly be good for his brother to be gainfully employed somewhere.

At the same time, pressure was building on Galileo's sister Livia to get married. It was expected of women that they would marry by the time they were in their twenties, but Livia was already past that age and was still unattached. If she did not marry and find someone to support her, she would

GALILEO'S MONEY

Imagine the confusion it would cause if every state in the United States had its own currency. In Galileo's time, different areas within Italy had their own monetary systems. The main types of currency that were in use at the time were lire (divided into soldi and denari), florins, ducats (Venetian money), crowns, and scudi (Tuscan money). In 1606 Galileo wrote a manual on how to use his military compass (sector). One use he explained was as a calculator to convert currency. These were the values of some of the various currencies according to Galileo:

1 Venetian ducat = 6 lire and 4 soldi

1 Venetian ducat = 0.775 Florentine scudi

1 Florentine scudi = 1.29 Venetian ducats

have no choice but to give herself up to the convent and become a nun, because there was really no place in society at that time for an unmarried woman.

Livia herself did not like the idea of spending her life in the convent (where she was living at the time). Her mother, Giulia, made it a point to search until she found a husband for Livia who was of equal status as the Galileis.

Just as Michelangelo was about to leave for Poland, Galileo's mother wrote of a proposed match for Livia. Galileo wrote a letter back to his mother

Galileo, probably in his 30s.

asking her to hold off any wedding plans. Galileo had to provide Michelangelo with money and clothes for his long journey, and it would cost 200 crowns, which was a considerable sum of money. They said their goodbyes, and Michelangelo was finally off on his journey.

Though he was finally rid of the obligation to his brother, there was no way Galileo could afford to pay for a wedding now. Livia was getting anxious to leave the convent, and Galileo tried to soothe her. "Tell her," he wrote to his mother, "that there have been queens and great ladies who have not married till they were old enough to be her mother." A delay of a few weeks would be helpful, because at that point Galileo felt "Michelangelo will without fail send me a good sum of money." Michelangelo was supposed to pay part of his sister Livia's dowry, now that he had a paying position.

The match was made, and Galileo wrote to his brother, explaining how he had borrowed money to make a down payment on the large dowry of 1,800 ducats. Though Galileo waited, Michelangelo never sent the long-expected money. Galileo did not let this stop him from making sure Livia was taken care of. She was his sister, after all, even though the money was a strain on his finances.

Perhaps Galileo wanted to ensure that Livia made a good impression on her future husband, who was the son of an ambassador in Rome. He paid a great deal of money for gold bracelets, fancy shoes, gold and silver trimmings, velvet, and damask for her wedding outfit. The wedding clothes were very important, and were a way to let everyone who saw the bride know that her family could afford the best fabrics.

After the wedding was over and several months had passed, Galileo wrote his brother a letter saying how disappointed he was in him for not being responsive: "Though you have sent no answer whatever to any of the four letters which I have written within the last ten months, I nevertheless write.... If I had imagined things were going to turn out in this manner, I would not have given the child in marriage."

Michelangelo simply did not believe it was his duty to help provide for his family. In a letter a few years later, he wrote to Galileo that the debt he owed for Livia's wedding was going to be impossible for him to pay:

> As to my finding 1,400 crowns, which is the sum still remaining to be paid, I know I cannot do it, and never shall . . . You should have given our sisters a dowry . . . in conformance with the size of my purse . . . The idea of toiling all one's life just to put by a little money to give to one's sisters!

After his initial six-year appointment as a professor at Padua had expired, Galileo was reelected for another six-year term. Luckily for Galileo, his friend and supporter Giovanni Francesco Sagredo (1571–1620), an eccentric man with a large collection of animals in his palatial Venice home, asked the Senate for an increase of Galileo's salary. He was now to receive 320 florins, less than the 350 florins Sagredo had hoped to win for him. The smaller increase was probably due to the influence of Galileo's enemies, those who were jealous of him, and those who were unhappy with his attacks on the theories of Aristotle. One man even called for Galileo to resign and leave if he was unhappy with his salary at Padua. Aware of the tension in the situation, Sagredo warned Galileo not to expect any further raises for some time.

Meanwhile, Galileo's own social life was becoming complicated. Though he never married, Galileo met a young woman with whom he developed a romantic relationship. While living at Padua, he often made trips into the city of Venice. It was there, through his friend Sagredo, that Galileo met a young Venetian woman named Marina Gamba. Marina moved in with Galileo and became pregnant. Their first child, a girl, was born in 1600 and given the name Virginia (see page 74). Next came Livia in 1601 (probably named after Galileo's sister), and then lastly came the only son, Vincenzio (see page 107), in 1606. When Galileo left Padua in 1610, he took his daughters with him and left his son behind with Marina. Marina Gamba later married another man, named Giovanni Bartoluzzi, but Galileo remained friendly with the mother of his children.

AN·IMPORTANT·PUPIL

IN 1601 Galileo became the math teacher for a very important pupil. Of course, he had already taught a great many students by this time and was an experienced professor. This student, however, was not simply another face in a crowded lecture hall. This pupil was the son of one of Galileo's patrons, the grand duke of Tuscany, Ferdinand I de' Medici. The young boy, only about 11 years old at the time, was named Cosimo II de' Medici (1590–1621). Galileo could not refuse the favor asked of him by Ferdinand because he knew that his patron was already 52 years old, and that one day the son would succeed the father and himself become the grand duke. This was Galileo's chance to make a favorable impression on both father and son.

So, Galileo privately taught the boy mathematics, going through the basic principles with him and making sure the boy understood what was being taught. The eager learner tried hard to please his tutor, and Galileo tried to praise his student. The two seemed to get along well; this close contact with the young Cosimo II helped build a friendship that would last a lifetime.

❉ THE MEDICI FAMILY

The Medici family of Florence was a powerful and important group of bankers, princes, and patrons of the arts who ruled the city almost continually from the 1420s to 1737, when the line died out. The family was closely connected with Galileo for many years.

Aside from dukes and princes, the Medicis also included two queens of France—Catherine (1519-1589), wife of Henry II and regent for her son Charles IX; and Marie (1573-1642), second wife of Henry IV and regent for her son Louis XII, whose daughters became queens in Spain and England. The Medici family included cardinals and popes as well, such as Clement VII (1342-1394), Leo X (1475-1521; a great patron of the arts in Rome), and Leo XI (1535-1605).

The family was wealthy and influential but was still considered a friend of the common people. It began to grow rich through commerce and banking in the 13th century, and one Medici served as *gonfaliere*, or standard bearer, a high ceremonial office, of Florence. The family's influence fell with the banishment of Salvestro de' Medici (1331-1388) in 1382, until it was restored years later.

The family's true founder was Giovanni di Bicci de' Medici (1360-1429). He made the family the wealthiest in Italy, and perhaps all of Europe. He was made *gonfaliere* in 1421. Political influence followed the amassing of great wealth. Son Cosimo il Vecchio de' Medici (1389-1464) was considered the true ruler of Florence and voted "Father of the Country" by the people following his death. Cosimo was patron to such great artists as Donatello and Lorenzo Ghiberti, and he amassed the largest library in Europe, the Laurentian Library. Florentine life flourished under his rule, becoming the cultural center of Europe and the cradle of the new humanism, a movement involving the study of classical art and civilization.

Cosimo's grandson Lorenzo (1449-1492), called "the Magnificent," was a poet and patron of the artists Michelangelo and Sandro Botticelli, among others. He was considered Italy's most brilliant Renaissance prince, and under him Florence surpassed its own previous cultural achievements.

Catherine de' Medici, queen of France and grandmother of Christina de' Medici, wife of Grand Duke Ferdinand, Galileo's sponsor.

Continued on next page . . .

The Medici Family—continued

Lorenzo's son Piero (1472–1503) was expelled from Florence, but the family was restored to power in 1512 with Lorenzo (1492–1519), son of Piero. He ruled from 1513 under the guidance of his uncle Giovanni (Pope Leo X). After a series of unsuccessful leaders, Cosimo I (1519–1574) took power in 1537. He doubled Florentine territory, and Tuscany was transformed into a powerful region. Among his many achievements was the creation of the Accademia della Crusca (Academy of the Cross), which was in charge of promoting the Tuscan language; this is the standard Italian spoken today.

Lorenzo de' Medici, "the Magnificent."

In 1569 Cosimo was named grand duke of Tuscany. Power was concentrated in a new office building, called the Uffizi, where he also began a small museum. He bought and enlarged the Pitti Palace as his residence and built a private corridor between it and the Palazzo Vecchio, where the government met. It was in the year of Cosimo's death that Vincenzo Galilei moved his family from Pisa to Florence; this included 10-year-old Galileo.

Cosimo's son Francis I (1541–1587) was a weak ruler. His brother Ferdinand (1549–1609), a cardinal, was made grand duke in 1587, and was a more effective leader. He was greatly interested in science and appointed Galileo as professor of mathematics at the University of Pisa in 1588. Ferdinand married Christina of Lorraine (1565–1637), granddaughter of Catherine de' Medici, queen of France. Christina favored Galileo, and he wrote his letter on science and scripture to her. Ferdinand and Christina's son Cosimo II (1590–1621) ascended the throne in 1609. He offered a court position to Galileo, his former mathematics tutor, in 1610. Galileo dedicated *Starry Messenger* to him and his family.

Cosimo II's son Ferdinand II (1610–1670) was only 10 when he was made grand duke, and decisions were made by the two grand duchesses, his mother Maria Magdalena of Austria (sister of

Pope Leo X, Giovanni de' Medici.

Holy Roman Emperor Ferdinand II) and his grandmother Christina of Lorraine. Ferdinand could not protect Galileo from the Inquisition in 1633. Ferdinand and his brother Leopold established the Accademia del Cimento (Academy of Experiment) in 1657, a forerunner of scientific academies. The Tuscan economy slowed, and under Ferdinand II, his son Cosimo III (1642–1723), and his grandson Gian Gastone (1671–1737), both the Medici family and the city of Florence lost power. Gian Gastone erected a memorial to Galileo in the church of Santa Croce and placed his remains there. Gian Gastone left no male heirs, so the house of Medici died with him.

THE·THERMOMETER

As a man of a curious nature, Galileo noticed everything. He saw that even in the smallest and most unexciting occurrences there were observations to be made. The laws of nature were everywhere just waiting to be found, in every particle of every solid, liquid, and gas that made up the earth. Even the water he drank and the air he breathed were of interest.

There was great power in nature, Galileo observed. The wind, the lightning, and the raging rivers all had tremendous force. Being a man who loved to invent, Galileo wondered if the physical reactions of liquids and solids could perhaps be harnessed and put to some practical use. He knew that when the temperature of water rose to a boil, the water bubbled enthusiastically, and when it sank to freezing, the water turned to solid ice. Heat could have a definite impact on the way liquids behaved. This information could be useful in measuring temperature.

In about 1602, Galileo invented a thermoscope, the precursor to the modern thermometer. He took a glass bottle with an egg-sized bulb and a long, thin neck and rubbed the bulb in his hands until it was warmed. Then, he dipped the mouth of the bottle into a container with water, hand still attached to the bulb. Once the mouth of the glass tube was in the water, he removed his hand from the bulb. The water in the neck instantly rose up a few inches above the surface of the water in the vessel. As the glass cooled, the water fell back. This was a very crude invention, since liquid mercury was still years away from being used in thermometers. Other scientists continued to improve on this invention that Galileo first conceived in its early stages.

Later, Galileo invented a different kind of thermometer—a long, wide glass tube with smaller glass bulbs suspended inside, each containing a different liquid. The different densities of the liquids caused each of them to float at a different level in the water.

(LIQUID DENSITY)

WATER (LIQUID) is more dense than air (gas). That means if you were to weigh 1 cubic inch (16 cu cm) of air, it would weigh less than 1 cubic inch of water. That is why when you pour water into a cup, it remains on the bottom, below the air. But all liquids are not the same density. This is the principle that Galileo applied to his thermometer.

MATERIALS
* ⅓ cup (80 ml) water
* ⅓ cup (80 ml) cooking oil
* ⅓ cup (80 ml) pancake syrup
* Glass measuring container

What do you think will happen when you put these three liquids into one container? Which will be on top? Pour the cooking oil into a glass. Now, pour the water into the same glass. Observe what happens: the oil rises to the top. Now, pour the maple syrup into the glass. Where does the syrup wind up? Which one do you think is the most dense of the three liquids?

✦ STAR MAGNITUDE

For centuries, astronomers viewed the stars in the sky. Ancient Greeks and others who followed cataloged the stars. They thought that the fixed stars never changed, according to Aristotle's view of the universe. In 1572 and again in 1604, "new stars" suddenly appeared that were so bright they caused astronomers to reconsider Aristotle's propositions. Through careful observation, Maestlin, Brahe, Kepler, Galileo, and others were able to prove the distant stars were not unchanging.

Star magnitude (level of brightness) has to do with the size and age of a star, as well as its distance from the earth. Sometimes what looks like a bright star is actually the planet Mars or Venus. If you go outside on a clear night, you'll notice that each star is a different brightness. Astronomers developed a system to assign stars a magnitude based on their brightness. The brightest stars are a 0 or -1 value under this system. The values are not to scale, however. A star that is a 0 magnitude is 2.5 times brighter than a star that has a magnitude of 1, and a 0 magnitude star is 100 times brighter than a 5 magnitude star. The new star of 1604 was about -2.5 in magnitude, truly outshining any other star in the sky. What are the brightest stars you can find in the sky? How many stars can you find that are very dim, just barely visible?

NEW·STAR·OF·1604

Though he was too young at the time to make any scientific observations about the new star of 1572, the star that first appeared on October 9, 1604, most certainly caught Galileo's attention. The star, visible in the constellation Serpentarious, appeared to change color, at times seeming to become yellow, red, purple, or white. It was brighter in the night sky than even the planet Jupiter when it first appeared, before becoming duller and then disappearing altogether in a few months.

Galileo gave three lectures on the subject of the new star to a huge crowd of students and curious onlookers. The lecture hall became so packed that the hundreds of attendees were jammed in with hardly any room to move. Galileo was forced to take his lecture outside into the open so the audience members would not suffocate. Clearly, Galileo was gaining a solid reputation as a brilliant scientist.

After some commotion, when everyone was in their places and ready to listen, Galileo proceeded to explain to the crowd how the absence of parallax, an optical phenomenon that makes objects appear in a different location when viewed from different places, meant that the new heavenly object was not a meteor (a particle of rock that burns when it enters the earth's atmosphere), but was a star, and was far, far away. Elsewhere in Europe, other scientists such as Kepler were also coming to the same conclusion. In fact, the new star of 1604 came to be known as Kepler's Star.

THE·CAPRA·CONTROVERSY

In 1607 Galileo published a new booklet in Venice. The pamphlet was called *Difesa di Galileo Galilei Contro Alle Culunnie ed Imposture di Baldassar Capra*

Milanese (*Defense of Galileo Galilei Against All Slander and Pretenses of Baldassar Capra, of Milan*). A former student of Galileo's was claiming to be the inventor of the sector, and had even gone so far as to write a manual called *Usus, et Fabrica Circini Cujusdam Proportionis* (*Use and Fabrication of the Proportional Compass*). Baldassar Capra (1580–1626), the son of a nobleman, did not stop there. He also disputed Galileo's observations on the new star of 1604. This outraged Galileo, who could not let himself be taken advantage of.

Galileo began his written defense by saying that he could not believe how someone so well born and bred of honest morals could be guilty of such reckless slander (false charges). In the pages that follow, he tried to expose Capra's lies about the sector. He also went over the reasoning behind his observations about the new star of 1604. He backed this up with a detailed list of journal entries from many observers of the new star of 1572 that had appeared in the Cassiopeia constellation. These observers were from different countries and included Maestlin (Kepler's professor), Brahe, Gasparo Peucero, Paulo Hainzelio, Cornelio Gemma, and others. Galileo explained the findings of the scientists, and pointed out how Maestlin did not observe parallax, showing that the new star was very far away.

By this time, Galileo was already an expert at using his skill of self-defense. It was a skill that would be useful as his career progressed. As his discoveries grew in importance, so did the jealousy of those professors whose egos he had wounded. Now he also had to be prepared for people to claim his inventions as their own.

❊ THE PARALLAX PHENOMENON

Parallax is an optical phenomenon that makes objects appear in a different location when viewed from different places. You can test this out very simply. Stand about 6 feet (2 m) away from a television screen. Hold a salt shaker about 6 inches (15 cm) away from your face, so that it is framed by the screen. Close your right eye and observe where the salt shaker appears to be. Now, close your left eye and observe. The salt shaker appears to move in relation to the screen in the background, depending on which eye is open. The television screen, being farther away, does not appear to move much. This is the same principle that was applied by scientists to the supernovae of 1572 and 1604; there was no observable parallax because the stars were too far away.

Galileo Galilei, early 1600s (probably in his 40s).

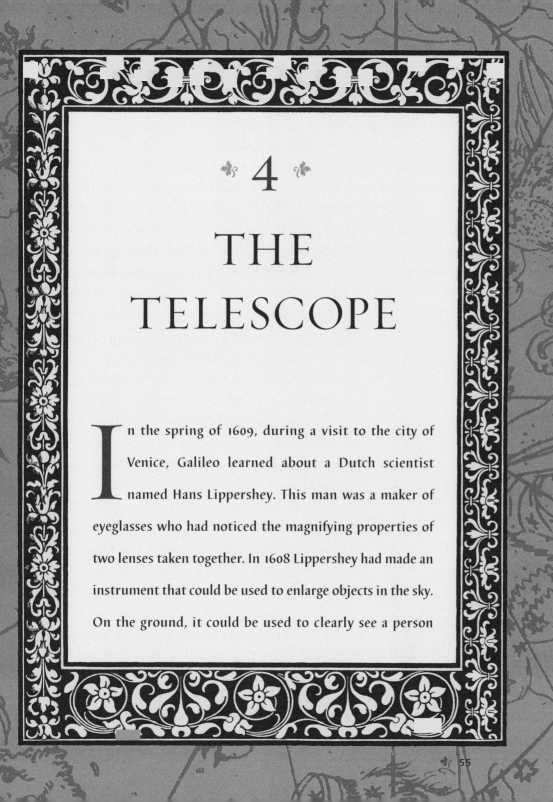

4

THE

TELESCOPE

In the spring of 1609, during a visit to the city of Venice, Galileo learned about a Dutch scientist named Hans Lippershey. This man was a maker of eyeglasses who had noticed the magnifying properties of two lenses taken together. In 1608 Lippershey had made an instrument that could be used to enlarge objects in the sky. On the ground, it could be used to clearly see a person standing 2 miles (3 km) away. Lippershey had presented one of these instruments to Count Maurice of Nassau. Galileo marveled at the thought of such an invention and wondered how it might be made.

When he returned to his home at Padua, Galileo turned his attention to creating a similar optical instrument that would magnify the heavens. He used two eyeglass lenses—one with a concave (curved inward) side and the other with a convex (curved outward) side. He put one lens at each end of a long metal tube. When he looked through the concave side, he was able to see objects that were magnified several times. Galileo brought the invention (which had the power of a pair of modern binoculars) to Venice and shared it with whoever was interested. Once word spread of the invention, Galileo was visited by crowds of people who were fascinated and wanted to have a look at the telescope. Important politicians, known as senators, climbed into the remote upper reaches of Venetian churches to look with the telescope into the harbor and see ships that were many miles distant. They had never seen anything quite like this wonderful new creation.

Leonardo Deodati, who held the title of the Doge of Venice, informed Galileo that the Senate was very interested in the invention. Galileo caught the hint and realized it would be a nice gesture to offer the telescope as a present, free of charge, to the Doge. Galileo wrote about this in a letter to his brother-in-law, Benedetto Landucci: "Recognizing the usefulness of such an instrument in naval and military warfare, and seeing His Highness's strong desire to possess it, I resolved four days ago to call at the palace and offer it to the Doge as a free gift."

The Doge's Palace in Venice.

After making his presentation of the valuable gift, Galileo was told to wait in the Senate Hall for a few minutes before leaving. Soon he found out the reason for the delay. An official of the University of Padua came out to meet him in the Senate Hall and told him some good news. The Senate was so pleased with the thoughtful and valuable gift that it had decided on the spot to give him a lifetime professorship as well as a 1,000-florin salary, a big raise from the 520 florins he was making before.

(APERTURE EXPERIMENT)

GALILEO AND JOHANNES KEPLER were both fascinated with optics and studied the properties of light and lenses. In order to create a telescope, Galileo had to understand how to use the powers of light and take advantage of the properties of the eye. Leonardo da Vinci and others had demonstrated the properties of an aperture, or small hole, in something called a *camera obscura*. A camera obscura is a dark chamber with a tiny hole in one side or wall. When the hole is placed in front of a brightly illuminated scene, the scene is projected through the hole onto the far side or wall of the camera obscura. Early astronomers used this camera obscura to project an image of a solar eclipse without looking directly at the sun.

This activity demonstrates how images are seen through an aperture. By understanding how optics work, you can better understand the nature of the light coming from the planets and stars all the way to the earth.

MATERIALS
- 2 pieces of thick, white paper
- Scissors
- Pin

Fold the paper in half and cut a tiny triangle (¼ inch [½ cm] or less) in the center of the fold. When you open the paper, you will have a diamond-shaped aperture. Hold this diamond-shaped hole up to one eye and close the other eye. Observe how the closer you are to an object (a computer screen, for example), the less of it you will see in the diamond. What you do see will have the shape of a diamond. On the other hand, as you get farther away, you will see more and more of the object, until you are far enough away that the object is whole.

Next, poke a pinhole in the second piece of paper. You cannot see much from a close distance, but you can look outside at night and see the moon through the tiny pinhole. Though the moon is larger in the sky than a pinhole, you can still see the entire moon through the tiny hole.

This aperture experiment proves that each and every part of a luminous or brightly lit object or body transmits light rays in all directions. In this case, the light rays from the moon are being emitted in every direction, including into the tiny pinhole. Light can and will travel wherever there is an opening. Cameras, microscopes, and telescopes all collect and intensify light in order to make clear (and sometimes enlarged) images of objects. This simple principle of light rays coming through an aperture was refined by Renaissance scientists who figured out how to clarify and magnify the light once it entered the aperture.

Galileo's letter to his brother-in-law told of the enthusiastic reception his telescope received in Venice:

Many noblemen and senators, although of a great age, mounted the steps of the highest church towers at Venice, in order to see sails and ships that were so far off that it was two hours before they were seen steering full sail into the harbor without my spy-glass, for the effect of my instrument is such that it makes an object of fifty miles distance appear as large and near as if it were only five.

Of course, Galileo was not content just yet. He wanted to keep making more telescopes, sparing no expense to improve their magnification capabilities until they could magnify 20 times and more. When Galileo turned his telescope toward the moon, he immediately noticed the wonderful three-dimensional details of its surface that came to life before his eyes—the valleys and peaks, the dark areas and light points. He wondered if the moon could be host to some form of life.

There were areas that looked like oceans, but had no water. The shadows were especially telling. Galileo studied the way light hit the moon and the way the shadows danced across the surface unevenly at the line where the light half of the moon met the dark half. No, the moon was not smooth and perfectly round as had been thought: it had a rugged and textured surface. In June 1611 Father Christopher Grienberger (1561–1636), a Jesuit priest, wrote a brief letter to Galileo about the mountains on the moon. Galileo replied in September with a long letter demonstrating his methods. The discovery caused a rush of imitators. Others tried to study the moon and make their own observations. One such publication in 1611 was called *De Lunarium Montium Altitudine—Problema Mathematicum (Altitude of the Moon's Mountains—A Mathematical Problem)*. Meanwhile, the followers of Aristotle were offended at being told that the moon was not perfectly round and smooth.

Shadows on the surface of the moon show the surface is not smooth.

❧ HOW·HIGH? ❧

GALILEO WAS a firm believer in the power of mathematics to solve scientific problems. The special use of geometric angles and ancient mathematical formulas allowed a whole range of questions to be answered.

For example, Galileo was quite curious to determine the height of mountains on the moon. But how could something so far away be measured accurately? Upon some reflection, Galileo devised a fairly simple method. As an example, he drew a picture of the moon and cut it in half down the middle, representing the light (on the right) and dark (on the left) sides. The length of that line, called AC, was the diameter. He drew a mountain located at a distance of about 1/20th of the total circumference of the moon from the top point A. He labeled its highest point F. Rays of sunlight (EAF) were hitting this mountain peak, even though it was on the "dark side" of the moon.

He then drew a point halfway between A and C, which he called G. This point G was the center of the moon, and the distance AG was equal to half of the diameter AC.

The whole problem could be easily solved using the ancient Greek Pythagorean theorem:

$$A^2 + B^2 = C^2 \text{ in a right triangle.}$$

Without the telescope, these calculations would not have been possible. What else could be discovered using the telescope? Galileo was excited by the possibilities. When he turned his telescope toward the stars in the black night sky, he noticed that, unlike the moon, they did not become any bigger. They were still just twinkles of light. This observation confirmed that the stars must be very far away, farther than the other planets, which did appear

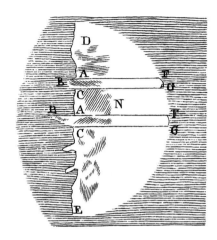

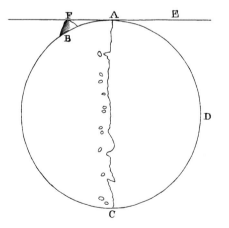

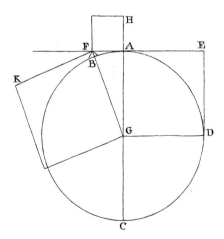

The two drawings at bottom show how Galileo determined the height of mountains on the moon. The drawing at top shows the shadows on the moon.

larger when seen through the telescope. Even while studying other heavenly bodies, Galileo never lost interest in the moon. He continued to make observations and discoveries about earth's closest celestial neighbor for the rest of his life.

Meanwhile, he continued to attract many admirers. Everyone wanted to obtain for themselves a "Venetian glass," as the telescope was known at the time. Still, not everyone admired his new invention and the discoveries he made. Other people were not so keen on Galileo's science. Some of these men who did not like Galileo were simply jealous of his genius and his popularity. Others felt his teachings and discoveries were false and went against what the Bible said.

MOONS·OF·JUPITER

EVERYONE HAS known about the existence of the earth's moon since the first humans roamed the earth because it is easily visible to the naked eye. Yet in 1600, no one knew anything of any other moons in the solar system. Another important discovery made by Galileo with his telescope was the moons of the planet Jupiter.

The first time he noticed something peculiar around Jupiter was in the middle of the night on January 7, 1610. Looking toward Jupiter with his telescope, he noticed what appeared to be three stars near the planet. On that night he saw two stars on one side of Jupiter and one star on the other side. He did not take any special note of it at the time, but then on January 8 he noticed that they were all on one side of Jupiter, nearer to one another than they had been the night before. They could not be fixed stars if they moved. What could this mean? The next night was cloudy, and Galileo was disappointed that he couldn't see anything at all. He waited until the sun went

✿ THE BIBLE AND THE PLACE OF THE EARTH IN THE UNIVERSE

The Bible does not actually say "the sun revolves around the earth," but it contains several passages that might be interpreted that way. The strict and literal view of the Bible's words by the Catholic Church in Galileo's time did not allow for any opinions that might contradict the exact words in the Bible. To make history fit the Bible, a bishop calculated backward based on the ages and descriptions given in the Bible, and figured out that the earth was created 4004 B.C.

With such a rich and complex book as the Bible, it is easy to support a particular idea with a citation of a few lines from one chapter or another. Views on almost any topic can be found in the Bible: what food to eat, the role of women, the rich versus the poor. Galileo and others were in the delicate position of finding that their discoveries went against the teachings of the Bible. For example, in the first chapter of the Old Testament you can find these words:

And God made two great lights; the greater light to rule the day [the sun], and the lesser light to rule the night [the moon]: he made the stars also.

And God set them in the firmament of the heaven to give light upon the earth, and to rule over the day, and over the night, and to divide the light from the darkness.

These words tell that the moon and sun and stars were all created for the benefit of the earth, just to keep it light. Anything that showed the heavens were not all in rotation around the earth was seen as blasphemy (against God).

Other examples from the Bible include:

Joshua 10:13: *"So the sun stood still in the midst of heaven."*

Psalm 104:5: *"Who laid the foundations of the earth, that it should not be removed for ever."*

Ecclesiastes 1:5: *"The sun also ariseth, and the sun goeth down and hasteth to his place where he arose."*

Deuteronomy 4:19: *"And beware lest you lift up your eyes unto heaven and when you see the sun, and the moon, and the stars, even all the host of heaven, should be driven to worship them and serve them . . ."*

Within this last passage is a warning not to worship or serve the sun or the stars. This may be at the root of why Galileo was in trouble with the Church. It was not just for suggesting that the earth revolves around the sun, but for being too much in awe of the heavens, studying them so closely, and disregarding the Bible and the word of God. Galileo also got into trouble when he tried to compare science with the Bible, as did a priest named Father Paolo Antonio Foscarini.

Bible leaf (a page from Genesis) printed in Venice, 1603.

Finally, Job 37:18 says: "Hast thou with him spread out the sky, which is strong, and as a molten looking glass?" This passage was cited by Galileo himself in a letter dated 1633 ("the sky is solid and polished like a mirror of copper or bronze") as one of many places in the Bible that seems to speak to the "ancient" theory, and as something that was used against him by the Church.

down on January 10, and that night he saw only two of the stars. The third was nowhere in sight. Again, he was perplexed.

The next night there were again just the two stars, but now one star was definitely bigger than the other! On January 12 the stars were again in different positions and appeared at a different magnitude. This was truly fascinating, thought Galileo. He was very happy to have this new instrument to examine the sky, because it was opening up a new world of wonders that had never been known before. These could not be stars at all, he imagined. They must be some type of secondary planets that revolve around Jupiter in the same way that Earth, Venus, Mercury, Mars, Jupiter, and Saturn revolve around the sun.

On January 13 he noticed for the first time a fourth star close to Jupiter. Of course, he could have ended his studies there, but being very thorough, Galileo felt the subject deserved a complete study. After concentrating on these new wonders for two months, he finally concluded his observations on March 22 and immediately began to write out his findings in book form. This work was exhausting, as it could only be done at night. Needless to say, he did not get much sleep during this time.

In honor of the grand duke of Tuscany, Cosimo II de' Medici, Galileo named the moons of Jupiter Sidera Medicea ("Medici's stars"). (The moons are today known as Io, Europe, Ganymede, and Callisto.) Eager to share his discoveries with the rest of the world, he published a book in the spring of 1610 called *Nuncius Sidereus* (*Sidereal*, or *Starry Messenger*). This book, which was dedicated to the grand duke, summarizes Galileo's observations of Jupiter's moons. The book was very popular and was immediately republished in Germany and France.

Even those people who had seen the moons with their own eyes did not know what to make of it. One doubter went so far as to suggest that Galileo's telescope somehow showed things that were not there, as if by magic. Galileo, his sense of humor and sense of outrage equally tickled, replied by offering a handsome reward to anyone who could make such a magical instrument. The discovery suggested that there were celestial bodies in the sky that most definitely did not revolve around the earth. They revolved around another planet! Whether people liked it or hated it, the book caused quite a stir and made Galileo very famous.

In a letter to his friend Kepler in August 1610, Galileo wrote

You are the first and only person who, even after only a preliminary investigation, has given whole credit to my statements, such is the openness of your mind and high genius . . . I think, my Kepler, we will laugh at the extraordinary stupidity of the multitude, for against Jupiter even giants, not to mention pygmies [dwarves], fight in vain . . . What do you say to the leading philosophers of the faculty here, to whom I have offered a thousand times of my own will to show them my findings, but who with the lazy stubbornness of a snake who has eaten his fill have never consented to look at planets, nor moon, nor telescope? Truly, as snakes close their ears, so do these men close their eyes to the light of truth.

Jupiter and its four Galilean moons.

Unfortunately, not everyone was so open-minded. A student of Kepler's named Martin Horky wrote a book against the discovery of the Jovian moons. He claimed that there were no logical explanations for these "planets" and that, in fact, Galileo had seen things that did not exist. All Galileo wished, according to Horky, was to gain fame and wealth and draw attention to himself. After Horky published the book, he was reproached by an angry Kepler. At Kepler's special request, Galileo did not bother to respond to Horky's ravings. Kepler asked that Galileo hold back from a reply, since it was beneath his dignity to do so. Instead, a former pupil of Galileo's named John Wedderburn (a Scottish man) wrote a reply called *Four Problems, that Martin Horky Proposed against the Four New Planets* (1610).

The discovery of new "planets" also upset the old-fashioned philosophy of the perfect and unchanging universe. An astronomer named Francesco Sizzi printed a treatise against Galileo's new discoveries, claiming in part that seven is the perfect number of nature: there are seven openings in the head (eyes, nostrils, ears, and mouth), seven days of the week, and seven metals. Sizzi said that there are also seven planets: Earth, the moon, Mercury, Venus, Mars, Jupiter, and Saturn. How could this perfection be broken? According to Sizzi, it could not. Anyway, if the naked eye could not see the new heavenly bodies, they did not really exist in any way that mattered.

A few years later, a German astronomer named Simon Marius printed a book in which he claimed to have discovered the moons of Jupiter first. Galileo knew this man had also been a part of the Baldassar Capra scandal. Galileo addressed this years later in his book *Il Saggiatore* (*The Assayer*):

> *This man, four years after the publication of my* Starry Messenger, *as usual wishing to adorn other people's hard work, did not blush to call himself the author of my findings published in that work, and printed with the title of* Mundus Jovialis *["World of Jupiter"] he had the temerity [daring] to assert that he had before me observed the Medicean Planets, that turn around Jupiter.*

THE · MOONS · OF · SATURN?

IN JULY 1610, having turned his telescope toward Saturn, Galileo became the first person to discover what we now know is a ring around the planet, though at the time he did not realize that was what he was seeing. To him it simply looked as if Saturn had two moons. Galileo sent word of this discovery out to his patron Cosimo de' Medici's secretary, Belisario Vinta. He also sent a clue about the discovery to the leading astronomers and mathematicians in

Italy and Germany, but he did it in the form of a confusing anagram that had to be solved to get the clue. (An anagram is a word puzzle in which the letters of a word or phrase are scrambled.) This would help keep his discovery from being claimed by someone else. The Capra controversy of a few years earlier was still fresh in his mind. He did not want to fight over his discoveries.

Such a difficult anagram might take some time to solve, time Galileo could use to make more study of Saturn before making an official announcement of the discovery. The anagram he sent went this way:

SMAJSMRMJLMEPOETALEVNJPVNENVGTTAVJRAS.

Kepler was happy to be part of Galileo's circle of trusted friends, but he found the anagram very difficult. He tried and tried to solve the puzzle, but all he could come up with was the Latin phrase "*Salve umbistineum geminatum Martia proles*" (which means "Mars has an offspring"); he thought the discovery had something to do with the moons of Mars.

Julian de' Medici, the Tuscan ambassador to Emperor Rudolf II's imperial court at the city of Prague, was asked by the emperor to get the explanation of the enigma. The ambassador wrote to Galileo with the official request, and Galileo felt he must not ignore it, coming from such a person of power. He supplied the answer in Latin on November 13, 1610: "*Altissimum Planetum tergeminium observavi,*" which means "The highest [farthest or uppermost] planet is observed to be tripled." By this he meant that Saturn, the farthest known planet at the time, looked, when seen through the telescope, like a large planet surrounded by two smaller planets on either side. When Kepler heard of Galileo's discoveries, they fascinated him. He longed to have his own telescope.

When Galileo sketched what he saw in his telescope, he drew a large *O* surrounded on either side by a small *o*. What Galileo did not know was that the "triple" effect he had discovered was actually Saturn's rings, which could be seen encircling the planet on either side.

✳ ANAGRAM

Galileo's announcement of his two discoveries in 1610 were in the form of anagrams. An anagram is a form of puzzle that goes back to ancient times. The letters of a word or phrase are scrambled. Sometimes the scramble is another word or phrase, and sometimes it is a big jumble of run-on letters, as was the case with Galileo's Saturn anagram. See if you can solve these two anagrams about Galileo and his discoveries. (Hint: they are both four words long and both contain the name Galileo.)

Sawagoeilgalsiune

Nduofglloeaisnmoospujreti

Answers: 1. *Galileo was a genius* 2. *Galileo found Jupiter's moons*

The rings of Saturn, seen from the *Voyager II* spacecraft.

Later in 1610 Galileo made another great discovery. He had turned his telescope toward Venus and Mars and saw that, when viewed in magnification, the planets appeared to have phases, just as the earth's moon did. Through the telescope, Venus had distinctly different shapes. It went from crescent phase to half phase to full phase. The new anagram he sent out in December 1610 to leading scientists and mathematicians, including his one-time pupil Benedetto Castelli (1578–1643), about Venus was

Haec immature a me jam frustra leguntur o ii.

This puzzle also had people stumped. In January 1611 Galileo sent out the solution. When the letters were rearranged, the new phrase was "*Cynthiae figures aemulator mater Amorum.*" The translation of that solution is "The Mother of Love [Venus] emulates [copies] the phases of Cynthia [Apollo, or the moon]." The importance of this discovery was readily understood by the genius Galileo. These planets rely on the sun for their light and must revolve around it.

STARRY·SKIES

FOR MANY HUNDREDS of years, astronomers used the existing catalog of stars created by Hipparchus in ancient Greek times. More recently, Tycho Brahe had also tried to catalog the stars, but also without the aid of magnification.

In the course of his careful observations of the heavens, Galileo turned his telescope toward some of the nebulae (galaxies or cloudy areas made of gas) in the sky and saw that they contained dozens more stars than were visible with the naked eye. The constellation Orion was made up of 500 stars, not a handful, as originally thought. He found 40 stars in the Pleiades constellation and discovered that the Milky Way contained numerous stars. Everywhere he turned his telescope, new stars were revealed. How far away must these stars be that they can only be revealed through magnification, Galileo wondered?

The very discovery of these "new" stars was in definite opposition to the old way of thinking, which held that there was nothing new to be learned in the skies. The catalog of stars would have to be revised. While the planets of our own solar system became tiny disks rather than points of light when observed through the telescope, all the stars visible with the naked eye still appeared to be only pricks of light. The planets must be much closer than the stars, and the universe must be much more vast than ever thought before, Galileo imagined.

To hear of such discoveries angered the supporters of Aristotle. They continued to claim that the telescope was trickery and refused to even look into it to see for themselves.

SUNSPOTS

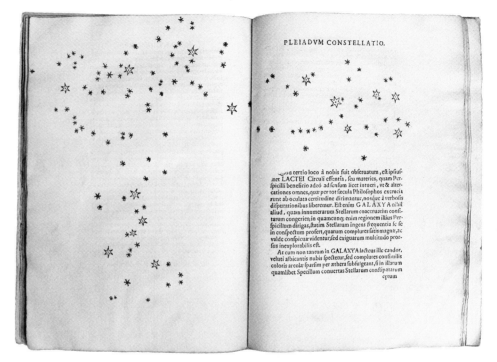

Stars Galileo observed in Pleiades, as shown in his book *Starry Messenger*.

ONCE THE TELESCOPE was invented, the science of astronomy progressed at an incredible pace. In March 1611 Galileo was able to view the sun through his telescope. With the help of his friend Castelli, he could use the telescope to magnify the sun and see the image without actually looking directly at it. In the course of his careful observations, he noticed that there seemed to be "sunspots," or locations on the sun that were darker than the rest of the surface. At first, he thought these spots were the dark sides of planets that revolved near the sun. Upon closer observation, he noticed

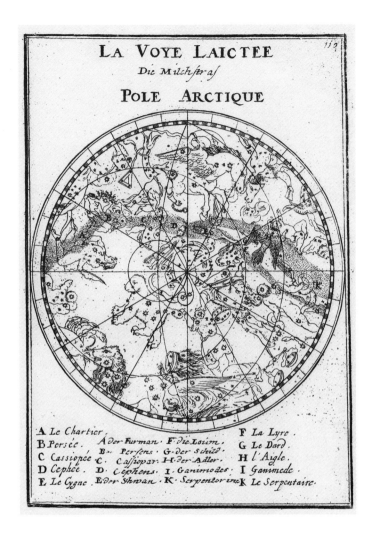

The constellations of the Milky Way shown in a 17th-century engraving.

that the spots were not regular shapes (the type that would be cast by a round object such as a planet). Then, he noticed that they were in fact spots on the surface of the sun itself.

There was some dispute as to who had discovered sunspots first and who had the correct interpretation. Kepler had actually noted a spot on the sun, which he thought was a planet passing in front of it. If he had made further study, he might have figured out that it was not a planet.

An Englishman named Thomas Harriott also noticed the sunspots around the same time as Galileo, in 1610 or 1611. It seems that Harriott first noticed the sunspots in December 1610, but did not make any real study of them until 1611. Another astronomer named Father Christoph Scheiner (1573–1650), a Jesuit professor at Ingolstadt University in Germany, claimed to be the first to discover the sunspots. He also believed the sunspots were the shadows of planets or other celestial bodies cast upon the sun. The Jesuits were conservative in their religious beliefs. Scheiner was determined to find an explanation for the sunspots that did not involve the sun being imperfect or subject to change. The sun must be perfect, according to Scheiner.

Scheiner's theories were printed in three letters he wrote to a patron named Marcum Velserum (also known as Marc Welser). These were published in 1611 as *De Maculis Solaribus Tres Epistolae* (*Three Letters on the Sunspots*). Scheiner wrote under the fictitious name Apellis Post Tabulam Latentis (Apelles Hiding Behind the Painting). He began the first letter by saying: "The phenomena, that I have observed and am announcing about the sun, is new and nearly incredible."

Welser asked Galileo for his comments on his theories. Galileo read the letters and disputed them in his response to Welser. The spots were most certainly not shadows, but were actually on the sun. After devoting some time to the study of the sunspots, Galileo tracked them by drawing their locations every day for some time. The spots changed in size and shape, and moved to different locations on the surface of the sun. They seemed to fade or vanish, sometimes after a couple of days, sometimes after a few weeks.

Galileo published his reply to the Scheiner letters in *Istoria e Dimonstrazioni intorno alle Macchie Solari e loro Accidenti* (*History and Demonstrations About the Sunspots and Their Properties*) that was printed in 1613 by the Lincei Academy.

Angered by Galileo's reply, Scheiner was now on the growing list of Galileo's enemies. Though years later he changed his mind and agreed with Galileo's theories about the true nature of the sunspots, he still disliked Galileo.

The various scientists who examined sunspots used a number of methods. Castelli had helped Galileo with a method in which the image of the sun was projected so that Galileo did not have to look at the sun directly. Dark-colored green or blue glasses could also be used to minimize the harmful brightness of the sun. Observing the sun when it was low on the horizon or behind very light clouds or mist was somewhat safer.

Christoph Scheiner's notes on the sunspots he observed in 1611.

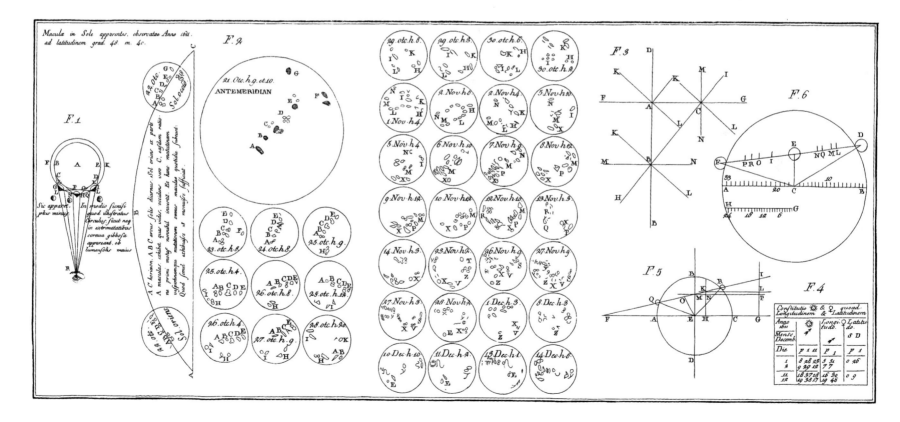

Though he had been pressured to resign from the university at Pisa years before, Galileo still longed to return to the region. Tuscany was his home and was quite a different environment from Padua and Venice. While still at Padua, Galileo had kept up his correspondence with the grand duke's family in Florence. In 1609 Galileo's patron Ferdinand I died and was succeeded by his son Cosimo II on February 7, 1609. At the time, Cosimo

(CAST A SHADOW)

AT FIRST, Galileo believed that the sunspots were shadows cast by nearby planets. Then, he noticed that the spots were not regular in shape. In this activity, you will look at the shadow of a round object and see what possible shape the shadows of a round object can cast. Compare these shapes to the sunspot shapes on the drawings on page 69.

MATERIALS

✳ Orange (as round as you can get)
✳ Knitting needle (at least 8 inches [20 cm] long)
✳ Piece of 30-by-40-inch (75-by-100-cm) foam board

✳ Flashlight
✳ Measuring tape
✳ Black magic marker or permanent marker (use caution with permanent marker)
✳ 2 friends

Poke a small hole in the orange and stick the knitting needle into the hole, so you can hold the needle and have the orange fixed to the end without it falling off. Lean the foam board against a wall so it is as close to parallel to the wall as possible. Have one friend kneel down and hold the needle with his or her arm extended in front of the foam board. Kneel in front of

the orange at a distance of 2 feet (60 cm). Shine the light directly at the ball at the same height. Have your second friend trace and color in the outline of the shadow.

Now, have the first friend move his or her arm slightly so it is in front of a clean part of the foam board. Change the angle of the flashlight, and have friend number two again draw the shadow that is cast. Do this a few times using different angles and distances. Compare the shadows you have observed to the sunspots seen in the illustration on page 69. Could sunspots be caused by the shadows of round planets cast upon the sun?

was only 19 years old. Galileo wrote a letter to a man from Florence named Signor Vespuccio:

It is impossible to obtain from a Republic, however splendid and generous, a stipend [fixed sum of money] without duties attached to it, for to have anything from the public one must work for the public . . . In short, I have no hope of enjoying such ease and leisure as are necessary to me, except in the service of an absolute prince . . . daily I discover new things, and if I had more leisure, and were able to employ more workmen, I would do much more in the way of experiment and invention . . . I am greatly assisted in the maintenance of the house by having pupils, and the earnings from private lessons, as much as I wish.

Galileo did not want Vespuccio to share the letter with anyone except for a trusted friend (who had been tutor to Cosimo II de' Medici) named Enea Silvio Piccolomini (1586–1619).

The young grand duke thought it would be quite an honor to have Galileo return to Tuscany and make his home there once again. The grand duke offered to negotiate with the scientist. Galileo was intrigued by the offer. Though he was fairly happy as a professor at Padua, the lectures and students took up too much of his time and interrupted him from his experiments and writings. If only he could have the time and freedom to write and publish at will, that would make it worthwhile. He promised to dedicate his writings to the grand duke.

A deal was reached, and Galileo resigned from Padua. The university officials were not very happy to lose their star professor, but eventually they forgave him for returning to his native land. His new duties would be light, consisting of lectures to princes and other members of royalty.

Most importantly, he would be able to write and publish books on numerous subjects in which he was interested but had not had time to investigate. He listed some of these subjects in a letter to the grand duke's secretary, Vinta, in May 1610. The list included two books about the system that constitutes the universe, three books on mechanics, and works about sound and speech, sight and colors, and the tides.

Galileo was also very interested in military strategy. He told Vinta that he wanted to write a book about all the ways mathematics could be used in warfare, including the construction of fortifications, military planning, weaponry, and surveying. Also, he added, he very much wanted to republish a book on the use of the geometric compass he had invented because "no more copies can be found." He had big plans and desired to be free of the academic chains that he felt bound him and made his days pass too quickly.

By the fall of 1610, Galileo was back in Pisa, and his new title was philosopher and "primary and superior mathematician at Pisa." Galileo was not officially affiliated with the university there. He was living largely off the good will of his patron.

Meanwhile, Galileo suffered from bouts of ill health and decided that the city air was partly to blame. Consequently, he spent much of his time at his friend Filipo Salviati's villa in the countryside, until his friend passed away in 1614.

VISIT·TO·ROME

As EXCITEMENT AMONG the community of educated men increased about Galileo and his discoveries, he decided to make a trip to the large city of Rome at the end of March 1611. Though Florence and Venice were beautiful old cities, Rome was the center of culture and history. It was the seat of power during the Roman Empire and was now the seat of power for the Catholic Church. It was the city from which legendary figures such as Julius Caesar had ruled the entire land during the great Roman Empire. The Colosseum and other landmarks were reminders of Rome's grand past and made it a city known and respected around the world. The Vatican, where the pope resides, was a symbol of the tremendous power of the Church.

Galileo's trip was paid for by his patron, Cosimo II de' Medici, and while there he visited with princes, cardinals, and other noble and important people. He stayed at the Medici Palace and at the ambassador's residence, among other places. When he made the journey to Rome, Galileo made sure to bring with him the best and most powerful telescope he owned. Once he arrived, he set up the instrument in the garden of the important Cardinal Ottavio Bandini, who held the position of dean of the College of Cardinals at one point. There, he showed an audience of cardinals and other religious leaders the newly discovered sunspots, the rings of Saturn, and the phases of Venus.

Even the nonbelievers and the jealous were curious to see his discoveries, and Galileo was very happy to indulge them. He was quite willing to give anyone who would listen an earful of opinions, facts, and ideas. This openness and apparent inability to restrain himself when dealing with potential enemies was typical of Galileo's behavior. He did not live in fear. He spoke his mind and answered anyone who questioned him.

Cardinal Francesco Maria del Monte wrote to Grand Duke Cosimo II in May of 1611 to proclaim Galileo's visit a success. He said that Galileo had satisfied those he visited and must have been very happy himself at having had the chance to show off all his great discoveries. The cardinal wrote: "Were we still living under the ancient republic of Rome, I truly believe that there would have been a column on the Capitol erected in his honor."

✤ GALILEO AND THE LINCEI

The Lincei was a scientific group founded in Rome in 1603 by four young scientists, including the son of the duke of Aquasparta, Federico Cesi (1585–1630). Eighteen years old at the time, Cesi was the leader of the group and became known as Prince Cesi. Though not actually a prince, he was in a sense the "prince" of the Lincei. The academy was partly inspired by the work and experiments of Galileo. The name "Lincei" is Italian for "lynx," a catlike animal known for its keen senses. The members of the society wished to pursue the natural sciences with a sharp eye toward detail and toward discovering the true nature of the world.

The academy added a prestigious member on April 25, 1611, when Galileo joined while visiting Rome. By 1625 there were 32 fellows of the society. Part of their function was to oversee the publication of their members' works. Among the studies they published were two of Galileo's works: On Sunspots in 1613 and The Assayer in 1623. The title page of The Assayer explains that Galileo was "the Primary Philosopher and Mathematician of the Most Serene Grand Duke of Tuscany and also a member of the Lincei Academy." The book was dedicated to Maffeo Barberini, who became Pope Urban VIII in 1623 and was also a member of the Lincei Academy.

Cesi's early death and the fact that the group had supported Galileo spelled the end for the academy. In the years that followed, the academy was reborn, died, and was reborn again several times. The present-day group is known as the Accademia Nazionale dei Lincei and is headquartered in Rome. Its aims are "to promote, coordinate, integrate, and spread scientific knowledge in its highest expression, in the unity and universality of culture."

AMID ALL THE great discoveries, Galileo was noticing that his little girls were growing up fast. By 1611 Galileo had decided to try to have his daughters admitted into a convent so they could spend their lives there. The monetary difficulties of seeing his sisters married still sat heavy in Galileo's mind. Though he loved his daughters very much, he did not envision himself taking care of them for several years and then paying for their dowries. Galileo thought himself to be a good and devoted Catholic, and he believed that the Catholic Church could take care of his daughters. In an isolated life as nuns, the girls' illegitimacy (meaning, according to Catholic Church rules, they were not officially Galileo's daughters because he did not marry their mother) would be irrelevant, whereas in public life their reputations might be stained, and it may have been difficult to find suitable husbands for them.

Galileo's wish was that both daughters be placed into the same convent, a request for which he had to receive special intervention because the pope was not in favor of the idea. Also, because the convent was already full, Galileo would have to pay extra to have them taken in. Most importantly, the girls were not old enough to become nuns, and the law forbade them from staying in the convent otherwise. In 1545, the Church declared that the minimum age for entering the convent would be 16 years old.

Though they were too young, Galileo received special permission from his ally Cardinal Bandini, and in October 1613 Galileo's two daughters entered the Franciscan convent of St. Matthew at a place called Arcetri (a short distance from Florence). The Franciscans were a well-respected order of the Roman Catholic Church that was founded in the 13th century.

The next year, in 1614, the two sisters "took the veil" and became nuns, though only 13 and 14 years old. The eldest daughter, Virginia (1600–1634), took the name Sister Maria Celeste, and the younger daughter, Livia (1601–1659), took the name Sister Arcangela. Virginia seems to have intentionally picked the name Celeste (meaning "heavens" or "sky") in honor of her father's interest in the skies.

Galileo's daughters did not enjoy an easy life in the convent. The lives of nuns were not full of rest and relaxation. There were prayers and other duties that had to be attended to. Different days featured special masses or prayers, depending on the time of year. While the convent was a refuge from the outside world, it was a world unto itself, with its own expectations, regulations, and difficulties.

Though she had the company of her sister Arcangela in the convent, Maria Celeste still missed her father. For the most part, all she had were the letters he wrote, which she treasured. She could not leave the convent grounds. Though Galileo was free to visit her and her sister, that only happened when he was feeling well enough to go out. By the time Maria Celeste was 22 years old, her father was already 60, and his health was declining.

Maria Celeste frequently asked about her father's health and was always sorry to hear when he was not feeling well. On one occasion, she wrote to her father with advice on staying well:

The only thing I am sorry to hear about is that you are in the habit of going into the garden in the morning. I cannot tell you how sad I am to hear this, for I feel certain that you are making yourself liable to just such another lingering illness as you had last winter. Do pray quit this habit of going out, which does you much harm; and if you will not give it up for your own sake, give it up for your daughters' [sake], who desire to see you arrive at extreme old age.

Maria Celeste and Sister Arcangela mended shirts for their father and did other sewing projects. Galileo sent his daughters supplies that they could not get at the convent; in one instance, Maria Celeste asked for a chicken from Galileo's yard. Maria Celeste sent her father homemade treats, including

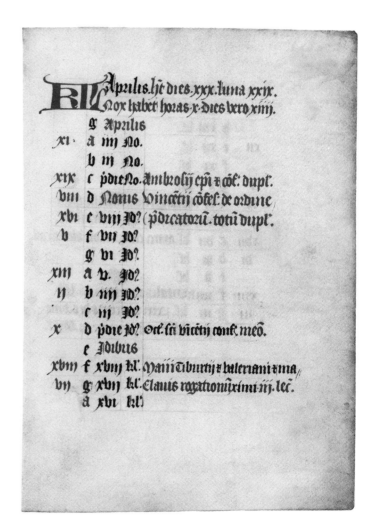

Page from a Renaissance-era church calendar for the month of April.

cakes and biscuits, whenever she could. On one occasion, she sent a rare "winter rose" that had improbably blossomed in the cold of mid-December. She wrote to him that with the rose, he must accept the thorns, and she compared the thorns to the death of Christ and the leaves to the promise of eternal life after death. Throughout his later years, Galileo viewed the numerous letters from his daughter as a constant reminder and support of his own Catholic faith.

The sisters suffered almost as many health problems as their father. The conditions in the convent were not at all ideal. Freezing cold and deadly drafts in the winter were replaced by intolerable heat and stillness in the summer. Fever and other diseases were common.

Though Galileo was their father, Maria Celeste and her sister were not "lawfully born" in the eyes of the Church because he and Marina Gamba never married. The two sisters had no legal claims on Galileo. Still, Galileo treasured his daughters, especially Maria Celeste, whom he said had "high mental gifts, combined with a rare goodness of heart."

FLOATING·BODIES·CAUSES·UPROAR

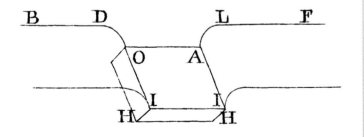

Illustration from *Floating Bodies*.

T HE ANCIENT GREEK scientists and philosophers had written on many subjects, including mathematics, physics, and astronomy. All of these were still taught at most higher schools and universities around Europe in Galileo's time.

Since his earliest days at the University of Pisa, Galileo had been interested in examining these old texts and putting them to the test. Galileo had long been interested in the properties of water and how objects float and displace water, a topic covered by Archimedes thousands of years before. Galileo wrote a pamphlet called *Intorno alle cose che stanno su l'Acqua, o che in quella si muovono* (usually known in English as *Discourse on Floating Bodies*). This work was dedicated to Galileo's patron, Cosimo de' Medici and was published in 1612.

In *Floating Bodies,* Galileo deflated some of the commonly accepted theories of Archimedes and Aristotle. Galileo carefully developed experiments to discover the true nature of how things float, and whether their shape and density make a difference. His work is full of complex illustrations that show the mathematics and physics behind the concepts he is explaining. Archimedes thought that the shape of an object helped determine whether it sat atop the water or sliced through it. Galileo discovered the principle of surface tension. Water molecules near the surface exert pressure in three directions: down and to either side. The water/air interface is a special place and special laws apply to it because there is surface tension that keeps the denser water separate from the lighter air above.

A roar of disapproval followed from those who were still insistent that the ancients had to be right. Tolomeo Nozzolini wrote his attack in a letter of several pages addressed to the archbishop of Florence, Monsignor Marzemedici. When Galileo read this letter, he wrote a reply directly back to Nozzolini, defending what *Floating Bodies* said.

Other quite lengthy attacks came from Lodovico delle Colombe and Vincenzo di Grazia. These attacks were so comprehensive and long-winded that they take up the entire Volume III of the series titled *Opere di Galileo Galilei* (*The Works of Galileo*). Though Galileo knew that he was right, and that the mathematical and physical equations were proof, it still annoyed him to be questioned in such detail and with such bitterness. He knew, as he read these attacks upon his work, that religion was not the only thing standing in the way of truth. He realized that the stubborn hesitation of people to let go of their ancient teachers was a big problem.

(FLOATING NEEDLE) EXPERIMENT

IN *FLOATING BODIES*, Galileo proved that there were other forces at play besides shape and density that helped determine whether something would float or sink. In one experiment, he showed that a metal needle could in fact be forced to float on water under certain circumstances—and not always sink, as Archimedes had written.

MATERIALS
* 2 needles
* Washtub or large bowl of water
* Facial tissue

Take one needle and hold it about 1 inch (2.5 cm) above the water. Now, let go of it. What happened to the needle? It sank. Next, take a tissue, and fold it in half so its short ends meet. Place the folded tissue very gently upon the surface of the water and immediately place the needle on top of the floating tissue. Observe what happens next! The tissue will sink in a few seconds, but what about the needle?

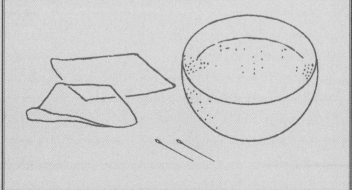

Though science and math were Galileo's main preoccupations, a lifelong passion for art was also a strong presence in his life. From the time he was young, he enjoyed painting and drawing. He drew his observations of the moon's surface and of the sunspots, among other things, in his notebooks. He was friendly with a well-known painter named Lodovico Cigoli, who had painted some very high-profile commissions, including the

(PAINTING LIGHT AND SHADOW)

GALILEO SHOWED that science could inform art. With his artistic eye, he was able to correctly interpret the surface of the moon as imperfect. In this activity, you will attempt to demonstrate the concept of *chiaroscuro* with your own imperfect surface.

MATERIALS
* Outdoor table
* Newspapers
* Sheet of 8½-by-11-inch (20-by-30-cm) white paper
* Piece of cardboard, at least 8-by-10 inches (20-by-25 cm)
* Piece of 8½-by-11-inch (20-by-30-cm) white cardstock

* Palette knife
* Black oil paint
* White oil paint
* Artist's paintbrush

Set the newspapers down on the table. Crumple the piece of white paper into a loose ball and set it down on top of the newspapers. Your goal is to try to paint the piece of paper so it looks three-dimensional. Examine the paper ball carefully. You will notice many shadows. Some shadows are darker and more defined than others. Use the cardboard as a palette and the white cardstock as a canvas. Squirt a little white paint onto the palette. Dab some white

paint on your paintbrush and paint the shape of the entire paper ball. Wait until this paint dries, then squirt some black paint onto the palette. Mix a drop of black in with the white paint, until you get a pale shade of gray that represents the lighter shadows. Paint those in next. When that paint has dried, create a darker gray paint, and use it to paint the darker shadows. Finally, repeat for the darkest recesses of the paper ball. The end result should be a three-dimensional representation of your paper ball showing the various nooks and crannies.

dome of a church in Rome and paintings on wet plaster known as frescoes in the palace of a cardinal.

Galileo became a member of the Accademia del Disegno (Academy of Design) in 1613. He was fascinated by the painting technique called *chiaroscuro* that Leonardo da Vinci had introduced. Earlier painters had used a two-dimensional approach to painting. Their paintings appeared flat and unrealistic because everything within the field of view was painted with the same degree of brightness.

The technique of chiaroscuro introduced the concept of light versus shadow to create depth and bring a third dimension into paintings. This use of chiaroscuro helped Galileo understand what he was seeing when he viewed the moon through his telescope. Instead of seeing two-dimensional dark spots on the surface, he saw shadows, which meant that the surface was not smooth, but was three-dimensional.

The painter Cigoli seemed to have incorporated Galileo's discoveries into his own work. In a painting called the *Assumption of the Virgin* (1612), Cigoli showed a moon at the feet of the Virgin Mary. The moon he painted looked three-dimensional, with craters and bumps, as Galileo had described it. Art and science had come together.

THE·SEARCH·FOR·LONGITUDE

SINCE ANCIENT TIMES, sailors set out in great sailing ships for trade routes across Europe, Asia, and Africa. They worried about getting lost, and so made sure to hug the coastline and keep land in sight at all times. By the 15th century, great voyages of discovery were taking place across the Atlantic and Pacific oceans. Even the greatest explorers only had limited tools to help them on the open sea. The best innovation in that era was the use of instruments that helped determine latitude, or how far north or south a ship was on the imaginary grid of lines parallel to the equator. By measuring the angle of the sun and stars above the horizon, sailors could determine if they were heading toward Brazil or Iceland.

The trouble was, there was still no way to determine longitude, or how far east or west a ship was located. Knowing latitude alone did not tell a ship's captain how much longer the voyage might take. Perhaps poor winds and bad storms had set him back several days. What if the crew was getting restless? Would the food supply last long enough? When would they hit land? Should they give up, turn around, and head home? The vastness of the oceans made determining longitude crucial to navigators in search of new worlds and new shortcut trade routes.

Several European governments offered prizes to the first person who could discover a reliable method to determine longitude at sea. The solution might have been simple. If there were a simple way to know the local time versus the time at the homeport—say Genoa, Italy—then longitude could be known. But that meant keeping clocks on board the unsteady, water-permeated ship that would keep accurate time. One clock would have to be set upon leaving the homeport, and one set at sea at noontime, upon observing the moment the sun reached its highest point in the sky. The bulky and inaccurate clocks of the day simply did not have the ability to last for weeks on end while keeping correct time. The difference of several minutes could throw off the longitude calculation considerably, and that would be both useless and disastrous, stranding a ship in the middle of nowhere.

Galileo enjoyed more than just philosophical questions about science. Ever since he was a child, he was eager to apply his ideas to practical inven-

A map from 1600 shows a ship sailing off the coast of Africa. In the days before longitude could be found at sea, ships hugged the coast as long as possible.

80

tions that could help people. The longitude puzzle was a tempting challenge for the genius. The offer of a prize added to the appeal of the puzzle.

Once Galileo discovered that the moons of Jupiter had eclipses, he was inspired. The whole plan began to form in his head. If he could make a chart of when the eclipses happened, a sailor could simply observe what time the eclipse occurred at sea, then refer to the chart to see when it was supposed to occur back at the homeport. By calculating the difference in times, the navigator could then figure out the ship's longitude. It seemed to be a perfect plan!

Galileo (through the grand duke) wrote a series of letters to Count Orso d'Elci, the Tuscan ambassador to Spain. He wanted to convince the Spanish government that his idea could work. The Spanish government was offering a generous prize that could make Galileo wealthy, as well as offering to the winner "grand honor and great recognition."

One letter explained that "in order to perfect the navigation on all seas, a method had to be found to find longitude, that in conjunction with latitude, the precise location on the terrestrial globe could be determined, at whatever point on the sea, the island, or the continent." And then, to begin the sales pitch, the letter goes on to explain what Galileo proposed: "The operation is infallible [incapable of error], and secure, depending on special motions of some wandering stars, that have been hidden from men until this age."

Discussions with Spain dragged on for years. Though he thought about the problem for a long time, Galileo was never able to come up with an acceptable way for the seamen to view the moons of Jupiter. An ordinary telescope would not be still enough at sea to focus on the tiny area of the sky where the moons could be found. Never one to give up without exhausting all possibilities, Galileo came up with another solution. He made a model telescope that was attached to a headpiece. Called a *celatone,* this instrument was put to the test in the waters off the coast of Livorno, but nothing further came of it.

In the end, Spain did not give the prize to Galileo, and his ideas were not developed until many years later (see page 146).

EVEN DURING his days at the University of Pisa some 25 years earlier, Galileo had made enemies because of his bold statements about the inaccuracy of some of Aristotle's scientific theories. As time passed, Galileo invented many wonderful instruments and observed and wrote about many new discoveries. Along the way, he continued to make new enemies.

Though individual enemies were powerful enough to have made him leave Pisa in 1592, they did not yet threaten his ability to work. Galileo still had many defenders, including well-connected royalty and religious leaders. Still, as he continued to prove that the Copernican theory was the correct model for planetary movement, priests began to take note of his ideas.

Galileo's friend Castelli was named as a professor of mathematics at the University of Pisa in 1613. When he accepted the position, he was warned that he had better not mention anything at all about the Copernican theory while teaching his classes. Castelli thought about it carefully and answered that no, of course he would never entertain the notion of teaching such a thing, and even his friend Galileo had advised him of the same.

Later that year, in December, Castelli wrote a letter to Galileo in which he told of a recent dinner party at the grand duke's residence in Pisa that he had attended. The dinner guests talked of the discovery of the new "stars" that revolved around Jupiter. One of the guests, a professor of physics and believer in Aristotle, admitted that this new discovery must be true. The proposition that the earth moved about the sun, however, could not be true, since it was against the Holy Scriptures. Castelli tried to be polite in his reply, and was on his way out the door at the party's end, when he was called back inside by one of the servants.

It seemed that Christina de' Medici (the mother of Cosimo II de' Medici) desired all the guests to be present as she made her own argument against Galileo's discoveries by using examples from the Holy Scriptures. She cited the passages of the Bible that seemed to contradict the discoveries of Galileo. How can Galileo be correct, she asked, when the Bible says otherwise in several places?

Galileo promptly composed a reply to the events recounted in the letter. He had thought carefully about the issues, and found a way to describe why he felt the Scriptures and science were two separate issues and did not contradict each other. In his heart, he was not against the Catholic Church. After all, he had placed his daughters in a convent because he trusted the Church to educate and care for them. To Galileo, it was simply ignorant for people to use the Bible as a way to disregard scientific truths. He wrote:

Though Scripture cannot err, any of its interpreters and expounders can err in various ways; one error would be most grave and frequent if we only accepted the words at their literal value . . .

And in the Scriptures can be found many propositions, that if taken in the bare sense of the words, appear to be against the truth, but they are put there in such manner for accommodating the common people . . . it is necessary for wise expositors to explain the true meaning.

The essence of Nature being inexorable [not to be moved or stopped] and immutable [not open to change], she cares not one bit whether her methods of operation are or are not within the mental capacity of men to understand . . . Natural effects that we see are not to be doubted because of certain parts of the Scripture that could be twisted into a thousand different meanings . . . Scripture is not bound by such severe laws as nature is ruled.

Two truths cannot be contrary to one another, so it becomes the job of wise expounders to work until they find a way to make these sacred passages agree with natural conclusions, of which either our senses or necessary demonstration have made us certain and sure.

I believe the authority of the Sacred Letters was to persuade men of the information needed for salvation . . . Astronomy is so little a part of the Scriptures that all the planets are not even named. If the sacred writings had been intended to per-suade the population about the disposition [nature] of the movement of celestial bodies, it would not have been passed over so completely.

Galileo felt that for theology to get involved in such matters would be like a king trying to instruct his subjects how to cure their sicknesses or to design buildings. The higher powers should stick with only the highest concerns and not try to deal with "lower" concerns about which they knew nothing.

Galileo's tone was firm in this letter. He seemed to be directly blaming those who would criticize him by telling them they had interpreted the Scriptures incorrectly. Though the letter seemed to state his belief in the Bible, he took aim at the "interpreters and expounders." This group could include monks, cardinals, and the pope himself.

He was really saying that nature was never wrong, but people could often be wrong. He was also saying that if the universe had been created by God, then that was the truth. If what people had thought in the past was proven to be incorrect, it did not contradict God, it simply showed the true nature of the universe the way God made it. People can be wrong (people such as Aristotle, for example), but God cannot be wrong. Galileo believed that God did not alter his creations so that the average person could understand them. Nature was there, in all its complexity and beauty, whether people tried to comprehend it or not. His argument was quite similar to the one that had been presented by the German astronomer Michael Maestlin (Kepler's teacher) in 1573. The heavens above were there, and by making new discov-eries about them, Galileo was not contradicting God.

Even further, Galileo turned the tables on those who quoted Scriptures to disprove the Copernican theory. In his letter, Galileo singled out the pas-sage from Joshua that told of God freezing the sun in the sky and making the day longer. He went into scientific detail about how this technically could not be done if the universe operated under the Ptolemaic system, but made more sense if the universe operated as described by Copernicus.

Castelli loved the letter. He made copies and distributed them to friends, so it was not surprising that a copy of Galileo's inspired letter somehow found its way into the hands of his enemies. In particular, a group of Dominicans of St. Mark read the letter with great agitation. What could be done? It was sheer heresy (to speak or write against the Bible or the Church) to write such things. One of the Dominicans, named Father Niccolo Lorini, sent a copy of the letter to the Holy Office in Rome. He wrote that "the Holy Scriptures should not be mixed up in anything but matters of religion."

Though Galileo intended his letter to be a compromise, a scientific and philosophical look at the question of religion versus science, the Dominicans did not view it as such. Galileo himself wondered how the letter got into the "enemy" hands and thought that perhaps whoever copied the letter may have accidentally changed a word. "Such a mutation," he wrote, "may make things seem very different from my intentions."

On the last Sunday before Christmas in 1614, a Dominican friar named Tommaso Caccini (1574–1648) attacked Galileo and Nicolaus Copernicus viciously as he gave a sermon at the church of Santa Maria Novella in Florence. He mocked Galileo by quoting from a passage from the Acts of the Apostles in the Bible: "Ye men of Galilee, why stand ye gazing up into heaven?" Though in the Bible, the men were looking into the sky as Jesus disappeared into a cloud after delivering a message to his followers, the reference to Galilee was meant to be a sarcastic play on words referring to Galileo and his followers. Caccini also ranted that all mathematicians should be banished from Christian countries because they are evil.

The tide of opinion among many in the Church was beginning to turn against Galileo. The enemies he had made over the years were happy to join in the attack. Galileo was not content to sit back and let himself be attacked by ignorant fools. Though he was no politician and certainly had none of the powers that cardinals and princes had, he was a man of ideas, and he had always been bold enough to share them. The ravings of Caccini and the Dominicans were getting to him. He felt he must respond with the truth.

RIONE

DI

MONTI

P. du Sel

Palais Baberin

S.t Jean de Latra

Monte Cabala

Colise

R.

CAMMPITELLI

Capitole

R. COLONNA

Rodarle

Minne
R. PIGNA

R. MARZO

ANGELO

R. EVSTACHIO

Marana Ruisseau

P. Borghese

R. PABIANE

R. REVOLA

P. Farnese

C.t S.t

R.

FONTE

RIONE DI RIP

Ang
o du
hasteu

R. DI
BORGO

S.t Esprit

Tibre

Vatican

S.t Pierre

RIONE DI

TRASTEVERE

Pertusa

P. de

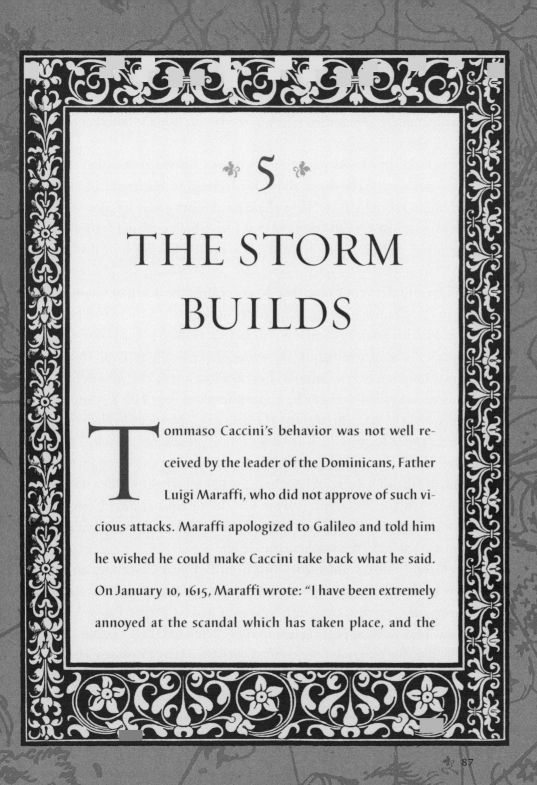

5

THE STORM BUILDS

Tommaso Caccini's behavior was not well received by the leader of the Dominicans, Father Luigi Maraffi, who did not approve of such vicious attacks. Maraffi apologized to Galileo and told him he wished he could make Caccini take back what he said. On January 10, 1615, Maraffi wrote: "I have been extremely annoyed at the scandal which has taken place, and the

Nicolaus Copernicus at work.

more so because the author of it is a brother of my order; for, unfortunately, I have to answer for all the beastliness which 30 or 40,000 brothers may and do actually commit." Nonetheless, it was too late to stop the ball that had begun to roll toward Galileo.

Though the attack was partly on Nicolaus Copernicus, Galileo took all of it very personally. He wrote about his feelings to his friend Monsignor Pietro Dini in February 1615: "Now these good friars, solely because of a sinister feeling against me and knowing that I have high esteem for this author [Copernicus], are proud to reward his work by having him declared a heretic."

Galileo found it very ironic that 70 years after the death of Copernicus, people in the Church were speaking badly of him, when there had been no problem with his book up to that point. In fact, Galileo pointed out, Copernicus himself was very religious. He wrote emphatically to Dini: "Nicolaus Copernicus was not only a Catholic, he was also a monk." He also noted that Copernicus was called to Rome by none other than Pope Leo X, a supporter of science and the arts who wanted the help of Copernicus in changing the Church calendar because he was viewed as a *"grandissimo astronimo"* ("great astronomer"). It was only logical: if the pope had been so strongly against Copernicus's theories, he would not have asked for his help. Galileo was upset because he felt the declarations from Caccini's pulpit against Copernicus were not just a declaration against a single person and his theories, but against mathematicians and even mathematics itself.

On March 7, 1615, Galileo got word from Federico Cesi about an excellent new book, *Lettera sopra l'opinione de'Pittagorici e del Copernico* (*Letter About the Pythagorean and Copernican Opinions*), by a man named Father Paolo Antonio Foscarini. This work, appearing just in time, defended the Copernican theory while showing that it did not conflict with the Holy Scriptures. However, later that month Galileo heard from another friend that it seemed Foscarini's book was bound to be banned by the Church because it dragged the Scriptures into the picture.

On March 19 the Dominican Caccini was called to Rome to give testimony about Galileo. There, he was free to spread rumors and lies about Galileo and made the most of the opportunity. He said that Galileo believed that the saints did not perform miracles and that suspicion should be aroused because Galileo belonged to the Lincei Academy. Caccini told how he heard from a priest some of the blasphemous things that Galileo's followers said.

Another Dominican, named Father Niccolo Lorini, who was a professor in Florence, publicly denounced Galileo and his followers on February 5, 1615. He said: "All the fathers of this convent of St. Mark find many passages in this letter which are suspicious or presumptuous as when it says that many expressions of Holy Scripture are indefinite . . . that the Holy Scriptures should not be mixed up in anything except matters of religion." Lorini also proclaimed that the followers of Galileo were too clever and conceited, and had tread upon the entire philosophy of Aristotle. Other rumors flew around about Galileo: that the grand duke was now against him, and that Galileo was guilty of more than just heresy.

Cardinal Mellini requested the original letter that Galileo wrote to Benedetto Castelli in 1613, because all he had was a copy of it. Castelli had returned the letter to Galileo, who wrote another copy and sent it to Castelli. Galileo had asked his friend to not, under any circumstance, let the letter leave his hands. So, Castelli read the letter out loud but refused to give it up. Galileo meanwhile made another copy of the letter and sent it on to Monsignor Dini, asking him to share it with a Jesuit priest named Christopher Grienberger, who was a mathematician and a great friend and patron to Galileo.

Galileo's friend Cesi advised him to be very careful: he had heard that Cardinal Roberto Bellarmino (1542–1621) thought the Copernican theory was heresy. Yet Galileo heard from a contact in Rome that it seemed to be acceptable to Cardinal Francesco Maria del Monte if he spoke of the Copernican theory, as long as he stayed away from the Holy Scriptures and left that to the preachers. Of course, Galileo knew that what he was trying to do was show that his theory did not conflict with the Scriptures.

❊ GALILEO'S HUMILITY

Though he was forceful in proclaiming scientific truths and in defending himself against his enemies, Galileo was also very humble to those who were his friends and patrons. The manners of the time required him to behave so. When he dedicated his works to the grand duke or other noble persons, he heaped a lot of praise and honor upon them.

In his letter to Monsignor Dini in 1615, Galileo began with a greeting to his "Most Illustrious, Reverend, and Honorable Lord" and closed the letter in this way: "With this I reverently kiss your hands, I remain your most devoted servant and to the Lord God I pray that he grants you great happiness."

In a letter to the Archduke Leopold of Austria, he closed with: "I kiss your clothes with all due reverence."

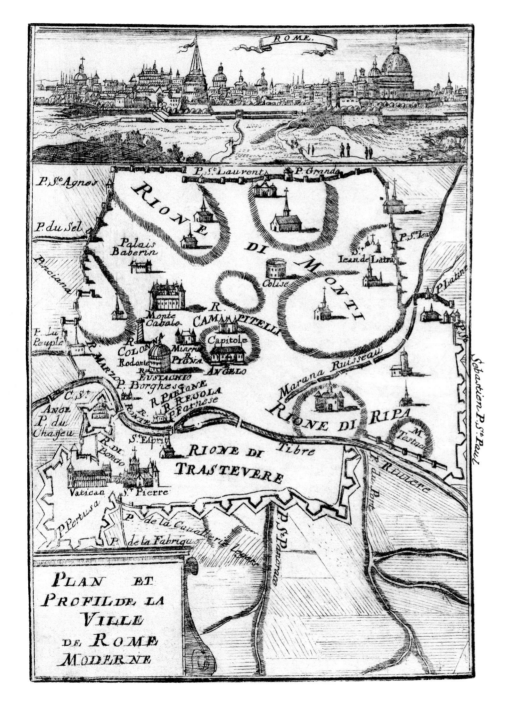

He decided not to hide himself away, but to go directly to the hotbed of rumors and controversy and visit the holy capital of Rome. Grand Duke Cosimo II de' Medici wrote a letter to Cardinal del Monte on November 28, 1615, explaining that Galileo was "deeply aggrieved by the calumnies [misrepresentations] that have been spread by certain envious persons" and had therefore "resolved to go to Rome, and has asked my permission, having a mind to clear himself from such imputations [accusations]."

ADMONISHED BY·THE·CARDINAL

Like a hungry lion, the general uproar that Caccini and Lorini had started had to be satisfied. On February 19, 1616, the qualifiers of the Holy Office (the qualifiers were a panel of "experts") were given two propositions. Their job was to decide whether these two propositions were true or false:

I. The sun is the center of the world, and immovable from its place.

II. The earth is not the center of the world, and is not immovable, but moves, and also with a daily motion.

The Holy Office pondered these questions and decided they were false, absurd, and wrong in faith. Therefore, they

◀ **Panoramic view of Rome seen from the surrounding countryside.**

decided to make an official pronouncement that teaching the theory of Copernicus was not allowed. A decree was issued on February 25 calling for Galileo to appear before them. Galileo appeared before Cardinal Bellarmino in Rome on February 26, 1616. The decree read:

> *In the usual palace home of Lord Cardinal Bellarmino . . . the said Galileo having been summoned and brought before the said Lord Cardinal . . . was ordered and regulated in the name of the Pope and the whole office of the congregation of the Holy Office, to totally [give up] the said opinion that the sun is in the center of the world and immobile and earth moves, nor otherwise to maintain, teach, or defend verbally or in writing; otherwise against him the Holy Office will proceed: to that order the same Galileo [gave in] and promised to comply with. Done at Rome, in the place aforementioned, in the presence of Badino Nores, of Nicosia in the kingdom of Cyprus, and Agostino Mongardo of the Abbey of Rose, diocese Politianen, inmates of the said Cardinal's house, witnesses.*

On March 5, 1616, the Congregation of the Index (the group that was in charge of selecting books to be placed on the index of banned books) issued a decree that took an official stand about the Copernican theory. In the decree, the work of Pythagoras, Copernicus, and Diego de Zuniga were all named as contrary to the Holy Scriptures.

Another work was particularly troublesome to the Congregation of the Index. This book was written by a member of the Carmelites (an order of Catholic friars), Father Paolo Antonio Foscarini (1565–1616), and was titled *Letter of Reverend Father Master Paolo Antonio Foscarini Carmelite, on the Opinion of the Pythagoreans and of Copernicus concerning the motion of the earth, and the stability of the sun, and the new Pythagorean system of the world* (printed in Naples in 1615). He repeatedly mentioned the sun, moon, Earth, and the planets (Mercury, Venus, Mars, Jupiter, and Saturn), and spoke of the mystery of their true nature. He mentioned how the telescope had revealed "a variety of sensational, beautiful

✦ THE HOLY INQUISITION

The Inquisition was begun during the Middle Ages as a sort of court for trying people suspected of committing heresy. It was a way to control the religion and protect against the many sects, or offshoots, of the Church that were appearing. In 1233 the pope established a formal Inquisition through which organized investigations were made in various parts of Europe. During the 1500s the Inquisition was also a way to battle the new threat of Protestantism. Ultimately, though, what the Inquisition sought was to get the suspected heretics back into the arms of the Church so they would be good Catholics.

After a grace period, if the person suspected of heresy did not confess and recant, a secret trial was held. Those who were tried were sometimes tortured. The finding of guilt could lead to penance (the convicted heretic had to say special prayers for a period of time), fines, imprisonment, or even burning at the stake.

In 1542 Pope Paul III created the Congregation of the Holy Office to oversee all matters of faith. It was this Holy Office that dealt with Galileo.

things in the sky, all curious, and unknown until this century: how the moon is mountainous, and Venus, and Saturn tri-bodied, and Jupiter quatri-bodied, and in the Milky Way, and in Pleiades, and in nebulae are a multitude of great stars, and the new fixed star, and new planets, and new worlds."

Besides emphatically summarizing all Galileo's new discoveries, Foscarini made the mistake of trying to make the Copernican theory fit with the Bible. He referred to numerous passages of the Old Testament in his book. In one instance, he takes the opening line of the Bible: *In principio creavit Elohim Coelum, es Terram* ("In the beginning God created the heavens and the earth") and examines the meaning of each word. Did the word *Elohim* ("God") refer to the singular or the plural? Did it refer to the Holy Trinity or to one all-powerful being? He was looking for loopholes, ways to find in the Bible what the Church had not seen.

Galileo's friend Cesi liked the book, but the Index was outraged, first of all that a priest would write such a book and second of all at the nerve of taking on the question of the Copernican theory so directly. It was similar to the commotion over Galileo's now infamous letter regarding the arguments of Grand Duchess Christina in 1613. So it was decided: Foscarini's book was "altogether prohibited and condemned" by the Index. Any existing copies of this book would be destroyed.

Copernicus's controversial book *De revolutionibis orbium coelestium* (*The Revolution of the Celestial Orbs*) suffered a somewhat less severe fate. It would be suspended until reissued with "corrections." The Index objected to the passages in the book that spoke of the theory as science. They wanted those passages changed to indicate that the Copernican theory was only that—an unproven theory.

Galileo found this act by the Index to be ironic, considering that Copernicus had dedicated this now banned work to Pope Paul III when it was published in 1543. He felt very frustrated by the whole situation. Galileo could not get details, but he knew conspiracies were swirling about his own work and theories.

GALILEO STAYED in Rome to plead his case with the many powerful people there. As usual, he was thorough in his explanations and tried to convince his audience of the truth point by point. On March 11, 1616, Galileo met with Pope Paul V (1552–1621). Paul V was a very religious man, and observers said of him at the time: "The present Pope, is aware of his spiritual greatness, and how much deference and obedience should be shown to him by all Christian peoples."

During his visit, Galileo spoke to the pope about his enemies and the rumors they were spreading. The pope listened patiently and assured Galileo that he was highly esteemed, and that his critics were not of any consequence. Paul V told him: "You should not worry as long as I am pope."

On March 20, Curzio Picchena (the grand duke of Tuscany's secretary) wrote to Galileo and begged him to speak no more about the controversies surrounding him and the Copernican theory, and that he should return home. Galileo refused. Meanwhile, Piero Guicciardini (the Tuscan ambassador at Rome) was uneasy because the Pope Paul he knew was not open-minded and did not like educated men. Perhaps Guicciardini had in his mind the incident some years earlier in which Pope Paul had ordered a man named Piccinardi beheaded

Galileo demonstrating his system.

for writing an unflattering biography of a previous pope, Clement VIII. The work had never even been published, yet an informant told authorities of its existence. Though Paul V pretended not to care very much at first, rather suddenly one day, the poor man was taken and killed.

Galileo wrote to Picchena that he had acted very well and that he was behaving calmly and rationally, not giving his enemies any further ammunition to use against him. "I pray his highness to keep his good opinion of me until I return," he told Picchena.

Unfortunately, his evidence fell on deaf ears. The stir caused by the Dominicans was too strong to be ignored. A letter written by Guicciardini explained the situation:

> He [Galileo] has little strength or [judgment] wherewith to control himself, so that he makes the climate of Rome extremely dangerous to himself, particularly in these times, when we have a Pope who hates . . . geniuses . . . I for my part do not see what reason he has got for coming, nor what good he has gained by being here.

Another man who was in Rome at the time, named Antonio Querenghi, wrote that Galileo would argue with groups of 15 or 20 people at a time, all of whom were finding ways to poke holes in his theories. Galileo was heard in one Roman house actually supporting the claims of his opponents, agreeing with them and giving them a false sense of pride, only to then turn the tables on those arguments and knock them down with the facts of his discoveries. Though it was in the spirit of debate that Galileo was able to argue both sides of a point, his attackers must have felt quite embarrassed at being deflated in such a tricky way.

The Tuscan ambassador was not pleased that Galileo remained in Rome. Guicciardini did not want Galileo's presence in Rome to become an obstacle in the relations between the court of Rome and the government of Tuscany. Guicciardini felt strongly that Galileo could become an embarrassment to Tuscany if he remained at Rome any longer. On May 23 he wrote a letter to the scientist: "[His Highness] . . . would therefore be glad if . . . you would not tease the sleeping dog any more and would return as soon as possible. For there are rumors flying about which we do not like, and the monks [Galileo's enemies] are all powerful."

Galileo was mostly victim to rumors and whispers behind his back, spread by his enemies. He had heard all the rumors: that he had been punished, had been forced to do penance, and had been made to recant his theories. These false statements annoyed Galileo, and he finally asked that Cardinal Bellarmino write a letter to certify that, in fact, Galileo had not been at fault. The cardinal bowed to Galileo's request and wrote a brief letter on May 26, 1616. This letter would later become an important part of Galileo's trial before the Inquisition:

> We Cardinal Roberto Bellarmino having understood that Signor Galileo Galilei was calumniously [slanderously] reported to have in our hand abjured [renounced] and also was punished with salutary [beneficial] penance and being sought after to tell the truth that the aforementioned Signor Galileo has not abjured either in our hand or in the hand of any other person in Rome, or any other place that we know of, any of his opinions or doctrines, neither has he received any salutary penance, but only, the declaration made by the Holy Father and published by the Sacred Congregation of the Index, has been indicated to him, wherein it is set forth that the doctrine attributed to Copernicus that the earth moves around the sun, and that the sun stays in the center of the world without moving east to west, is contrary to the Holy Scriptures, and therefore cannot be defended or held.

Finally, in early June, Galileo heeded the advice of his good friend and supporter the grand duke and returned to Florence. That same month, Cardinal del Monte wrote that Galileo had left Rome with his reputation intact and had exposed the vicious lies of his enemies.

❀ LATIN

The Roman Catholic Church communicated in Latin. All European university students learned Latin, and many scholars still use Latin to write papers and communicate with one another. As you will see from this excerpt of Galileo's admonition (warning), many of the words are familiar because they are the source (or root) of modern English words. See how many of the bolded words you can identify in English. (Hint: Look at the English translation of the same passage on this page.)

*. . . quod sol sit **centrum** mundi et **immobilis** et terra **moveatur** omnino **reliquat**, nec eam de caetero quovis modo teneat, doceat, aut **defendat**, **verbo** aut **scriptis**.*

Galileo continued to suffer from various physical ailments that had begun years before. Some days he felt too ill to do anything except rest in bed. Aches, pains, and fever were common complaints. In 1617 he moved to a home called Villa Segni at a place named Bellosguardo near Florence. It was pleasantly situated atop a hill, and Galileo felt this would be better for his health. He was also pleased that the villa was less than an hour away from the convent where his daughters lived.

During this time, he also continued to study the heavens. But he was for the most part careful about what he said or wrote. He sent three telescopes and some of his writings on sunspots and the tides to a patron, Archduke Leopold of Austria (who happened to be the brother of the grand duchess of Tuscany) in 1618. In the letter that accompanied the items, he explained that he had written them a couple of years earlier, before the cardinal told him to abandon the Copernican theory. Since he was now aware of the trouble he could get into, he told the archduke: "I consider it a poem or a dream, and desire that your Highness may take it as such . . . but even poets attach value to one or another of their fantasies, and I similarly attach some value to this fancy of mine." Galileo also wanted to circulate his writings in case someone else advanced the same theories and claimed them as his own. That way, they would know "it is I who first dreamed this chimera [illusion]."

For the next few years, he was at times busy, and also at times ill. During this period, though he had moved back to Florence, Galileo was still in touch with his dear Venetian friend, Giovanni Francesco Sagredo. Hearing of Galileo's continuing sickness, Sagredo had advised Galileo to enjoy life and forget about the stars in the sky. "Let fools be fools," he suggested. But Galileo could not stop his mind from constantly working. When three new comets lit up the night skies in 1618, the 54-year-old Galileo was bedridden with a severe illness that left him very weak. The real illnesses he had were worsened by hypochondria. Every ache and pain was taken by him to be the sign of a serious, possibly life-threatening problem. Nervousness itself could contribute to his ill health by causing a general uneasy feeling.

Archduke Leopold visited the sickly Galileo and, perhaps wishing to lift Galileo from the doldrums of his sickness, asked that he attempt to make some observations about the new comets. Galileo, inspired by the request of his patron, did so with the help of his pupil Mario Guiducci, who put the notes Galileo made together into a clear form. Guiducci gave a lecture to the Florentine Academy on the subject, and published the notes in 1619 under the title *Discorso Delle Comete* (*Discourse on Comets*). The lecture began with poetic words about "the marvelous fabric of this universal machine of the world."

In the process, the writing contradicted some of the ideas of a Jesuit priest named Horatio Grassi (1585–1654). Grassi was offended by this work of Guiducci, and felt sure that Galileo was in fact behind the attack on his theories. In a carefully thought-out response, Grassi published a book called *Libra Astronomica, e Filosofica* (*Astronomical and Philosophical Balance*) under the pen name of Lotario Sarsi, and in it mentioned Galileo by name numerous times. Galileo was not at all pleased when he read this book. His temper flared, and he became quite enraged.

He pondered what to do next. Should he let Guiducci respond, since the work in question was under his name, and not Galileo's? Would he be lowering himself to respond to Grassi? In the end, Galileo decided that he must himself reply to "Sarsi." Because of his ill health, it took a couple of years to prepare the manuscript for a work called *Il Saggiatore* (*The Assayer*), which was finally published in the autumn of 1623.

The work was written in the form of a letter to Monsignor Don Virginio Cesarini, who was the recently appointed *Maestro di Camera* ("executive

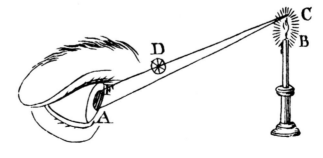

Illustration from Lotario Sarsi's book shows how the eye perceives the light of a candle that has been partially blocked.

assistant") of the newly installed Pope Urban VIII (see sidebar on page 101). In *The Assayer*, Galileo wrote very eloquently and thoughtfully, answering the points raised by Grassi over the course of several hundred pages, repeating word for word whole paragraphs from Sarsi's Latin work and then discussing each of Sarsi's points in Italian. At some points he seemed amused, at other points angry. But throughout, he tried to let the science speak for itself. In the course of the book, Galileo mentioned Sarsi's name more than 200 times!

Much of the dispute between the two men dealt with the way light is perceived by the eye, and how magnification of an object with the telescope affects the way it is perceived. Even though it was not one of his most important scientific works, it was well written and argued. In one passage, Galileo explains how science and math must be understood:

> *[Sarsi] thinks that Philosophy is a book, and a fantasy of man, like* The Iliad [epic poem by the ancient Greek writer Homer] *and* Orlando Furioso [an epic poem that Galileo liked very much, written by Ludivico Ariosto in the early 16th century], *books where the least important thing, is if that which is written, is true. Signor Sarsi, matters are not like that. Philosophy is written in that grand book that continually opens in front of our eyes (I mean the Universe) but we cannot understand it, if we do not first learn the language and know the characters in which it is written. This is written in the mathematical language, and the characters are triangles, circles, and other Geometrical figures, without whose help it is humanly impossible to understand a single word, and without which one goes around in vain in a dark labyrinth.*

Though Galileo tried not to be too controversial, the Jesuits took great offense to the work. Galileo had attacked one of their own. The leaders of the Jesuits issued an order that forbade members of the Jesuit order from discussing *The Assayer* amongst themselves. From that point on, Galileo had another powerful enemy to contend with. Despite all this, the pope was said to enjoy having *The Assayer* read to him at meals.

❧ LEARN ITALIAN

Most of Galileo's masterpieces were written in Italian. Below, you can learn a few of the key words that appear again and again in Galileo's writings. Pronunciations are given in parentheses. Many of the words may sound familiar because both English and Italian use many words with Latin roots.

astronomia (ah strohn oh MEE ya) — astronomy

cardinale (kar dee NAH lay) — cardinal

chiesa (kee AY zah) — church

cielo (chee EL oh) — sky

Copernico (ko PEAR nee ko) — Copernicus

Dio (DEE oh) — God

eclisse totale della Luna (eh KLEE say toh TAH lay DEL lah LOO nah) — total eclipse of the moon

filosofia (fee loh so FEE yah) — philosophy

Fiorentino (fee or ehn TEE no) — Florentine

Firenze (fee REN zay) — Florence

Giove (jee OH vay) — Jupiter

gran duca (grahn DOO ka) — grand duke

grandissimo (grahn DEE see moh) — great, very good

illustrissimo (ee loo STREE see moh) — illustrious

lettera (LEH teh rah) — letter

libri (LEE bree) — books

Luna (LOO nah) — (the) moon

macchie (MAH kee ay) — spots (on the sun)

Marte (MAR tay) — Mars

matematici (mah tay mah TEE chee) — mathematics

Mercurio (mehr COO ree oh) — Mercury

monti (MOHN tee) — mountains

natura (nah TUR ah) — nature

nuova (NWO vah) — new

opera (OH pear ah) — works (writing)

osservazioni (ohs ayr vah zee Oh nee) — observations

pianeti (pee ah NEH tee) — planets

sacre (SAH kray) — sacred, holy

satellite (sah TAY lee tay) — satellites

Saturno (sah TUHR no) — Saturn

Scrittura (skree TUHR ah) — Scriptures

Sole (SOH lay) — sun

Stella (STEH lah) — star

telescopio (teh lay SKO pee oh) — telescope

uomo (WO moh) — man

Venere (VEH neh ray) — Venus

Look at these pages from Galileo's work *The Assayer*. How many words from the vocabulary list can you spot on the pages?

Pages from Galileo's *Assayer*.

(PERCEPTION OF ILLUMINATION)

GALILEO WROTE in *The Assayer* that the true shape of a star or planet could not be made out with the naked eye because the general aura of illumination obscures the shape. Even when Venus is in crescent phase, the naked eye cannot distinguish any difference. Once put under the telescope, the radiation of light disappears, and the true form of the body is shown. Galileo likens this to a radiant head of hair worn by the celestial body. From a distance, the "hair" dwarfs the size of the body. As he put it, the earth's moon is so large in the sky that it dwarfs its own radiant head of hair, and so we can see its shape clearly. In this activity, you will observe this "radiant hair" principle for yourself.

MATERIALS
* Wide-open outdoor space
* A friend
* Flashlight
* Binoculars

In the evening, after the sun has set, find a wide-open space. Have your friend stand about 5 feet (1.5 m) from you, turn on the flashlight, and shine it at you. Can you see the distinct circular shape of the light? Now, have your friend walk until he or she is 50 feet (15 m) away and then shine the flashlight again. Can you still make out the shape of the flashlight? Repeat by having your friend walk another 50 feet (15 m) away. What does the light look like now?

Use the binoculars to look at the flashlight. What happens to the image that you saw with the naked eye only when you put it under magnification?

The relative sizes and shapes of the planets seen through the telescope, from *The Assayer.*

THE·NEW·POPE

GALILEO AND HIS FOLLOWERS had high hopes when they heard that the next pope would be Gregory XV. However, after less than two years as pope, Gregory XV died on July 8, 1623. On August 6, 1623, Maffeo Barberini was selected for this powerful position. Barberini was a cardinal who was very well known to Galileo. The two had corresponded over the years, and Galileo had shared some of his writings directly with the cardinal.

About Galileo's work on floating bodies, the cardinal had written in 1612: "I have received your treatise on various scientific questions . . . and shall read them with great pleasure, both to confirm myself in my opinion, which agrees with yours, and with the rest of the world to admire the fruits of your uncommon intellect." In 1613 the cardinal explained how pleased he was to receive Galileo's letters on sunspots. Barberini told Galileo in a thank-you letter that he would make it a point to take some time off to read and enjoy the works: "It is not a book that should be left to sleep idly amid the other books," he wrote. He was so inspired that he wrote of looking forward to finding a telescope and observing the wonders of the skies—"if the telescopes we have here are good enough to suffice."

Cardinal Barberini was also a poet who enjoyed writing. He sent Galileo some Latin verses he composed in honor of the scientist. In the note accompanying the poetry, he wrote to Galileo: "The esteem that I have always had for your person and for your numerous merits have dictated the verses I have enclosed in this letter. If they are not worthy of you, at least they offer you a proof of my affection; I would like to contribute, if it is possible, to enhance the renown of a name so glorious."

These words must have rung in Galileo's ears for many years after, for they are the words of a true admirer. But Barberini was a complicated man, as Galileo would later find out. Despite his seeming friendship and support of Galileo's science, in fact, Barberini never actually said that he supported the Copernican theory. On the other hand, it was reported that he said about the decree: "Our intention was not to condemn it."

According to accounts of the time, Pope Urban VIII was very self-confident and even conceited. A report dated 1624 said about the pope: "He loves his own opinions, and allows himself to be flattered by his own genius, to which is added stiffness in holding his own ideas." Urban VIII once repealed a Roman law that no statue could ever be raised of a living pope, and once, when confronted with some old Church ruling, stated that whatever a living pope says is worth more than the decrees of 100 dead popes. He was an energetic and athletic man who demanded respect. He aspired to greatness and carried himself with great importance. He was also very fond of talking. An account from 1627 said the following about Urban VIII:

He abounds in great eloquence of discourse, and is copious [abundant] in reasoning on various things, he argues and treats in matters with all the arguments that he understands and knows . . . it has often happened that people who have gone in for the purpose of explaining their requests, as a consequence of him setting himself to speak, have come away without being able to say anything at all about their interests.

Another account tells of how the pope liked contradiction, and that one practically had to trick him by pretending to object to an idea or thing that

Pope Urban VIII.

was actually wanted, and in finding a way to oppose and contradict the objections, the pope would actually wind up agreeing with what was desired.

In the fall of 1623, Galileo's friend Cesi urged him to visit the new pope. "It would be in your best interests to pay Urban VIII a visit, to show your face and give your greetings," Cesi told Galileo.

Unfortunately, in August of 1623 Galileo had a serious bout of illness and suffered in his bed for many days, causing his daughter much worry about the state of his health. Though his health finally improved at the end of the summer, he was still weak. The pope's nephew wrote to Galileo to say that indeed the pope was eager to see him, but not if the trip would be too taxing on the scientist's health—"for great men like you must spare themselves, that they may live as long as possible."

As autumn turned to winter, terrible flooding made travel dangerous. Though he was eager to test his standing with the pope, Galileo decided he must wait until the weather improved before making the trip to Rome.

In the meantime, the very learned Cesi was keeping track of the attitudes of Urban VIII. While waiting for Galileo to visit the pope, he wrote that under the "learned" Pope Urban, science would most definitely flourish.

Galileo's daughter Maria Celeste was very pleased to hear about the new pope as well. She wrote in a letter to her father in autumn of 1623:

I cannot describe the pleasure with which I read the letters of the illustrious Cardinal who is now our high priest, knowing as I do how greatly he loves and esteems you. I have read the letters several times [Galileo apparently let her borrow letters sent to him by Barberini when he was cardinal] . . . May the Lord give you health to fulfill your desire of visiting his Holiness, so that you may enjoy a still greater measure of his favor . . . I imagine that by this time you will have written a most beautiful letter to his Holiness, to congratulate him on his having obtained the tiara [crown].

The scientist finally felt up to making the trip in April 1624. He first stayed for two weeks at Cesi's home in Aquasparta, and then continued on to Rome.

Galileo found the pope to be very receptive, and during the course of his two-month-long visit to Rome, he saw the pope six times. Urban gave Galileo gifts, including a silver medal. He promised a pension to Galileo and his son, Vincenzio. Being from Tuscany, Galileo was technically a "foreigner" and was not eligible for a pension, so the pension was really quite an endorsement for what Galileo represented. The pope also wrote a letter of praise to Ferdinand II (1610–1670), who was Cosimo II de' Medici's son and successor as the grand duke of Tuscany. In the letter, the pope wrote how Galileo deserved to be treated well by the new grand duke:

He is strong in those qualities by which [papal] good will is easily obtained . . . we have lovingly embraced him . . . And so that you may know how dear he is to us, we have decided to give him this honorable testimonial of virtue and piety. And we further signify, that every benefit that you shall confer upon him, imitating or exceeding your father's liberality, will lead to our thanks.

The pope's letter also said that he found within Galileo a profound love of science but also a sincere piety.

While in Rome, Galileo also visited with other Church officials, and got the distinct feeling that the Church was backing away somewhat from the strong position it took in 1616. In fact, when he was a cardinal, Barberini had not approved of the Church's position in 1616. The pope was supposed to have later said that the Church did not in fact condemn the Copernican theory, but only called it rash. Go ahead and prove the theory if you like, the pope challenged scientists, then perhaps it will not be viewed as rash.

All these things gave Galileo many reasons to be hopeful. Perhaps the new pope had turned the tide against the anti-Copernican sentiment. Galileo left for Tuscany with the feeling that Rome was not such a dangerous place for him anymore, and that he now had friends in the highest of places.

Meanwhile, Galileo continued creating new instruments. He had been working on another version of the telescope, one that could enlarge tiny objects from a close-up view. In December 1624, Galileo sent one of these *occhialini* ("glasses") to Cesi, accompanied by a letter that begins: "I am sending to Your Excellency an eyepiece to show the neighborhood of smaller things, of which I hope it is to your enjoyment and provides you with no small entertainment." Galileo also explains to Cesi how best to use this early form of microscope. (Though Galileo experimented with instruments for close-up magnification, the man who is credited with the invention of the modern microscope is Antonie van Leeuwenhoek, who made many biological discoveries by examining organic material under the lens of his microscope.)

MICHELANGELO·RETURNS

AFTER SOME YEARS in Munich, Germany, Galileo's brother, Michelangelo, decided that perhaps he should seek his fortune elsewhere. He was having trouble feeding and clothing his large family. He wrote to Galileo in 1627 and inquired about returning to Florence. In September 1627 he instead wound up sending his entire household to live with Galileo indefinitely. There was Clara, Michelangelo's wife, and his children, Mechilde, Alberto, Michelangelo, Cosimo, Anna Maria, and Maria Fulva. The only child missing was Michelangelo's son Vincenzo, who was in Paris at the time. Galileo agreed to pay to send him to Rome to study music. Vincenzo was taken under the wing of Galileo's friend Castelli, who soon found out how difficult the young man was. Castelli called Vincenzo stubborn, rude, wild, and vicious. Galileo tried to get young Alberto a spot in the household of the grand duke of Tuscany, but Michelangelo objected, claiming the boy was not old enough for such work.

Galileo's home at Bellosguardo was spacious enough that his sister-in-law and nieces and nephews could be comfortably accommodated. Galileo was in a position where his finances were not too strained by this extra burden.

(ROLL OF THE DICE)

BECAUSE GALILEO WAS a well-known logical thinker, his admirers sometimes gave him tricky mathematical problems to solve. Galileo was once approached with a particularly complicated mathematical problem.

Gamblers of the time used to bet on the outcome of the roll of three dice. They knew that rolling a 3 total or an 18 total was rare, because only one possible combination could bring each result: 1-1-1 or 6-6-6. But according to the way they figured it, there was an equal chance to roll a total of 9 as there was to roll a total of 10. Yet, in their experience, the number 10 seemed to come up more frequently as the sum of the three dice than did the number 9. Galileo's task was to figure out why this was so.

The way the gamblers explained their logic, there were six possible combinations that could result in a roll of 9: 1-2-6, 4-4-1, 3-3-3, 2-2-5, 2-3-4, or 5-3-1.

There were also six possible combinations that could result in a roll of 10: 4-4-2, 2-2-6, 3-3-4, 6-1-3, 5-4-1, or 5-3-2. So, how could more rolls come up 10 than 9? In this activity, you will attempt to see if more 10 rolls really do come up. This activity is done in several stages. Stick with it as Galileo did, and you'll learn a great lesson in probability (the chances of a particular event occurring).

MATERIALS

* 3 dice
* Notebook
* Pencil
* Calculator

Roll the three dice and chart the sum on a piece of paper. Repeat this process, writing down the result each time. After 100 rolls of the three dice, write

down the total number of times the number 9 was the sum and the total number of times 10 was the sum. Did 10 come up more frequently? It should have. Why?

Galileo examined this problem and saw that the answer lay not in the possible combinations, but in the total number of permutations, or possible outcomes of each roll of the dice.

Consider this question: When you roll one die, what are the chances you will roll a 6? What are the chances you will roll a 5? What about the other outcomes? When you have one die, you have an equal chance of rolling any of the numbers. No particular number has a greater likelihood of turning up than any other. There are six sides each with a different number from 1 to 6, and so each side has an equal

Continued on next page . . .

chance of coming up. However, things change when you roll two dice together.

If you roll two dice, there could be more than six possible outcomes. Each outcome does not have the same probability of occurring. With two dice, you could roll a 1-2 in two different ways. Either the first die could be 1 and the second die 2, or the first die could be 2 and the second die 1. So, you have two chances to roll a combination featuring the numbers 1 and 2. With the outcome of 2-2, you only have one chance. Both dice must roll 2. So, you have a better chance of rolling and coming up with 1 and 2 than 2 and 2.

For the first die that was rolled, there are six possible outcomes: 1, 2, 3, 4, 5, or 6. When taken together, the two dice have many possible outcomes: 1-1, 1-2, 1-3, 1-4, 1-5, 1-6, 2-2, 2-3, 2-4, 2-5, 2-6, 3-3, 3-4, 3-5, 3-6, 4-4, 4-5, 4-6, 5-5, 5-6, or 6-6.

But, as you have seen, it is not just the outcome that counts. A 3-6 can be rolled in two ways: as a 3-6 and a 6-3. Except for the doubles (1-1, 2-2, 3-3, 4-4, 5-5, or 6-6), the other combinations have two chances of coming up.

If you add the third die to the equation, this complicates things even more. Now, there are even more possible outcomes. Remember, each die has equal chances of rolling any of the six numbers. Each die should be treated separately in the equation. A roll of one 2 and two 1s can come up in these three dif-

ferent ways: 1-1-2, 1-2-1, or 2-1-1. In other words, the first die rolled could come up as a 1, while the second comes up a 1, and the third comes up a 2. This is one distinct outcome, or permutation. But you can also get a result of one 2 and two 1s if the first die rolls out to a 2 and the other two dice come up as 1s. This is another outcome.

Examine Galileo's problem again, and think about it in terms of outcomes:

Roll of 9: 1-2-6, 4-4-1, 3-3-3, 2-2-5, 2-3-4, or 5-3-1.

Roll of 10: 4-4-2, 2-2-6, 3-3-4, 6-1-3, 5-4-1, or 5-3-2.

True, to roll a 9 or a 10, there are six different possible sets of numbers. But there are more than six ways to roll those numbers. So, a roll that has a 1 and a 2 and a 6 can have many possible ways to show up: 1-2-6, 1-6-2, 2-1-6, 2-6-1, 6-1-2, or 6-2-1.

Each outcome has one each of 1, 6, and 2. For any of those rolls the sum will equal 9. Now, take the next two 4s and a 1, and you will see there are only three outcomes that will give you those numbers: 1-4-4, 4-1-4, or 4-4-1.

Now, observe that when you roll 3-3-3, there is only one possible way to roll it, because all three dice have to be exactly the same. The first die has to be a 3, as do the second and third: 3-3-3.

So, a combination with three different numbers (such as 1-2-6) can come up in six different ways. A

combination with two like numbers (4-4-1) can come up three different ways. A combination with all three the same (3-3-3) can have only one permutation.

Let's examine the combinations one more time, adding the num2ber of permutations in parentheses after each combination:

Roll of 9: 1-2-6 (6), 4-4-1 (3), 3-3-3 (1), 2-2-5 (3), 2-3-4 (6), or 5-3-1 (6) = 25 permutations.

Roll of 10: 4-4-2 (3), 2-2-6 (3), 3-3-4 (3), 6-1-3 (6), 5-4-1 (6), or 5-3-2 (6) = 27 permutations.

Therefore, there are fewer permutations in the outcomes that bring a total of 9 than there are in the outcomes that bring a total of 10.

(**Hint:** *If you have trouble understanding the concept of permutations, use three different colored dice to help you see the different outcomes.*)

Still, the ungrateful Michelangelo complained that his children were not being instructed properly. Though the trouble of caring for a large family was taking its toll on Galileo's health, Galileo still insisted that his brother's family would be better off staying in Florence. Michelangelo did not listen. "There is no remedy for this disorder except that I take my family back again. I must do it," he wrote in June 1628, "even if I have to come to Florence on foot." In August 1628 he made the long journey back to Florence to pick up his family. Galileo was not pleased. After all he had done for his brother over the years, he had received little thanks or appreciation for his efforts. Before Michelangelo died a few years later, he recognized that he had not been an ideal brother and begged for Galileo's forgiveness.

GALILEO'S·SON

VINCENZIO (1606–1649), the only son of Galileo Galilei, was born in Venice. Since his parents were not married at the time, he was considered to be illegitimate. In 1619 the grand duke of Tuscany, Cosimo II de' Medici, legitimized Vincenzio. When Vincenzio was 17, his sister Maria Celeste wrote to their father: "I recommend our poor brother to your kindness and I beg you to forgive him his fault in consideration of his young age . . . fearing you would find me tiresome, I can write no more, though I can never cease to recommend him to your favor."

Galileo's son was at times selfish, lazy, and stubborn. According to letters of his sister to their father, he was also a sloppy dresser. Vincenzio was a big spender who liked to live in luxury. In some ways, he was like his uncle Michelangelo. He studied law and math and got his doctoral degree, which was an expensive proposition for Galileo. To his credit, he did show a better

side. He visited his sisters at the convent and brought news of their father, which gave Maria Celeste some comfort.

Vincenzio relied upon his father and sisters to help keep him clothed. In 1628 Maria Celeste wrote to her father: "Vincenzio very much needs to have collars, and never thinks about it until he needs a clean one to wear. All those that he has are very old, and we have great trouble to fix them up. I want to make him four new ones trimmed with lace, and cuffs to match." Maria Celeste went on to ask her father to send either some material to make the collars or some money to buy the fabric. Another letter from Maria Celeste to her father, dated 1629, asked if either Galileo or Vincenzio had any collars that needed repairs.

In 1629 Vincenzio announced that he was going to marry Sestilia Bocchineri, a sister of one of Maria Celeste's best friends in the convent. When Maria Celeste and her sister Arcangela met the bride-to-be, they were pleased with her pleasant personality and also with the fact that she seemed to like Galileo. "What gave me the greatest joy was to see that she was fond of you," Maria Celeste wrote.

Maria Celeste also asked her father's opinion about the wedding present for the bride. She thought it might be nice to make Sestilia an apron; not only would it be a useful gift, it would also not be too expensive to make. She sent Galileo a list of ingredients needed to make several cakes and also asked her father if he thought she should make some chocolate biscuits for the occasion.

Vincenzio honored his father in 1630 when he named his first son Galileo. The next year, Sestilia gave birth to a second son, whom they named Carlo, and after that, a third son, named Cosimo. In 1631 Vincenzio was unemployed, and Maria Celeste urged her father to find him a job so that he might stay out of trouble and be less of an annoyance to Galileo, and so that "peace and quiet" might follow.

Though relations were somewhat strained between father and son for a few years, toward the end of Galileo's life it seemed his son was back in his good graces.

PLAGUE

FOR HUNDREDS OF YEARS, the deadly bubonic plague had ravaged the cities of Europe. Beginning during the 1300s, millions of people succumbed to the disease, which was spread by rats. During the 1600s, the plague was still going strong. It hit various parts of Europe in waves. In 1635 many German towns were hit particularly hard by the plague (known there as *pestilenz*), leaving only a third or less of the population alive. A particularly bad outbreak of plague hit the Florence area during 1630–31.

Because it was highly contagious, the plague set off panic wherever it struck. A large population of rats, combined with poor sanitary conditions in overcrowded areas, made the plague easy to spread. Disposal of the dead was dangerous. Those people who did not become infected often fled to the countryside or to unaffected locations elsewhere. Areas of isolation, called quarantines, were enforced so that the plague would not spread to other areas.

Galileo's son, Vincenzio, left Florence with his wife during the plague. They fled to a place called Prato, but they left their infant child behind with Galileo and his housekeeper, Piera, who helped keep everything in order. Galileo was angry with his son for leaving and not even staying in contact during the time he was away. Relations were strained between father and son for several months.

A glassblower employed by Galileo died from the plague in the autumn of 1630. This death worried Maria Celeste when she heard about it. She wrote to her father telling him to "spare no possible precaution against the present danger" and reminding him that the best remedy of all was "true contrition and penitence [sorrow for one's sins]" toward God.

Out of about 75,000 people in Florence, nearly 11,000 of them died during the outbreak of the plague. Normal daily life in Florence was not at

GALILEO AND HIS DAUGHTER sent each other many packages of food and other items over the years. Among the items that Maria Celeste sent her father were pastry, preserved citron fruit, spice cake, baked quince (a type of fruit), baked pears, and rhubarb.

Certain herbs, spices, and fruits have been known to have healing effects on the body. When Galileo was very sick, Maria Celeste sent him a healing tonic of vinegar, sugar, and pomegranate wine. She also sent him some cinnamon water, which was supposed to promote health, to help him feel better. Other mixtures of the time included preservative rosemary water, made with the fragrant herb.

Here, you will make a care package similar to what Maria Celeste sent to Galileo.

☾ *Adult supervision required*

INGREDIENTS AND UTENSILS FOR POMEGRANATE ELIXIR

* 6 ounces (170 g) pomegranate juice
* Drinking glass
* 1 tablespoon (15 ml) vinegar
* 1 tablespoon (15 ml) sugar

Pour the pomegranate juice into the glass. (If you have a fresh pomegranate, you can try to juice it yourself by squeezing or pressing the juice out of the seeds. But watch out: it could get very messy!). Add the vinegar and sugar. Stir it up well.

INGREDIENTS AND UTENSILS FOR CINNAMON WATER

* Pot
* 1 quart (2 pt) boiling water
* ½ teaspoon (2.5 ml) ground cinnamon
* ¼ cup (60 ml) sugar
* Strainer

Bring the water to a boil. Remove from heat and add the cinnamon and sugar, stirring the mixture together for a minute. Cool and strain. Now, try a sip or two of this concoction. How does it taste?

INGREDIENTS AND UTENSILS FOR PRESERVATIVE WATER

* 1 quart (2 pt) water
* Pot
* 1 ounce (28 g) white grape juice

* Petals of two roses
* Handful of rosemary leaves (from a grocery store or a plant nursery)
* Handful of sage leaves
* Peels of one lemon
* Strainer

Bring the water to a boil and add the grape juice, rose petals, rosemary, sage, and lemon peels. Boil for about five minutes. Cool to room temperature, then strain out the leaves and peels. Splash a little preservative water on your hands and arms. It may not fight disease, but does it at least smell good?

A 17th-century illustration showing pomegranates, which were used for medicinal purposes by Galileo's daughter. ➤

all possible during the plague, and trade slowed to a crawl. In 1630 the city of Milan was also ravaged by the plague, and many thousands died.

Doctors wore strange-looking outfits made of thick material such as leather, with a "beak" that held various aromatic herbs that were supposed to purify the air being inhaled.

Various remedies and preservatives were said to be effective against the plague. One formula said to boil rose water, wine, and elderflower water, and then add to that mixture various ingredients, including roots of angelica and bistort, leaves of sage and rosemary, wormwood, juniper berries, and lemon peel. Washing with this preservative water was supposed to help prevent someone from catching the plague.

Galileo's daughter Maria Celeste had her own version of a preservative against the plague. It was a baked food item and contained dried figs, walnuts, rue (flour and butter), and salt, mixed together with honey. She sent some to her father and told him to take a piece of it every morning with a little wine. She also sent Galileo a small sample of special strong water made by the abbess (the nun who ran the abbey).

A German text of the time described the positive effects of the pomegranate as a medicine:

From the pomegranate one presses a juice that is called in the apothecary [druggist] Vinum Granatorum [the Latin name for pomegranate wine]. Such wine is quite good on the inner heat of Plague-fever. So in with barley or sorrel water one mixes it and drinks it, then he lightens the thirst and cools the stomach heat.

Habit des Medecins, et autres personnes qui visitent les Pestiferés. Il est de marroquin de leuant, le masque a les yeux de cristal, et un long néz rempli de parfums

Doctor's plague protection outfit.

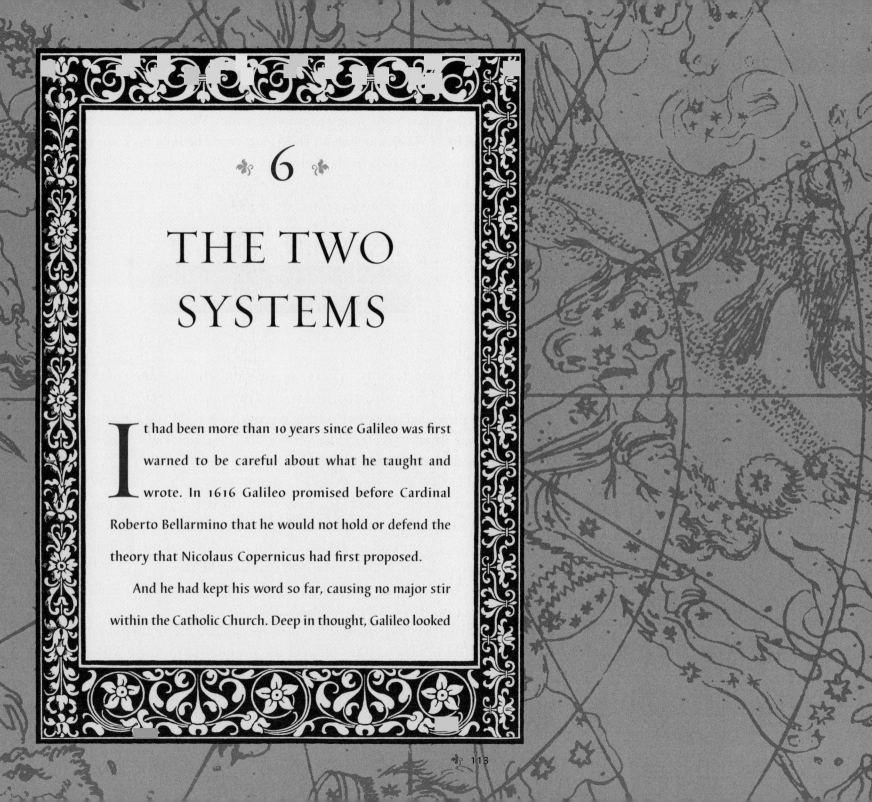

6

THE TWO SYSTEMS

It had been more than 10 years since Galileo was first warned to be careful about what he taught and wrote. In 1616 Galileo promised before Cardinal Roberto Bellarmino that he would not hold or defend the theory that Nicolaus Copernicus had first proposed.

And he had kept his word so far, causing no major stir within the Catholic Church. Deep in thought, Galileo looked to the horizon and saw the reddish glow of the setting sun. To most every-one, the sun's motion across the sky was proof enough that the sun moved around the earth. Something was gnawing at him. What kind of scientist was he if he had to keep quiet about this? How could he hold back any longer? Scientific truth is God's truth, he thought, and is just as sacred. He knew that he had to write the book he had wanted to write. The real question was how to accomplish this without getting into trouble.

GALILEO·PREPARES HIS·MANUSCRIPT

Galileo in his 60s or 70s.

GALILEO BEGAN TO WRITE, aware of the sensitive nature of the topic. To ease the controversy, he discussed the topic in the form of a dialogue among three characters (see sidebar on page 119). Galileo led his characters to debate whether the earth revolves around the sun, and whether it also rotates, creating day and night.

Galileo did not expect people to simply agree with his ideas. When he defended an idea, he used logic to advance the debate, to bring out all the proof he had and let the reader decide for himself or herself. In the end, the most logical arguments would have to win, and the ideas that still stood tall after a long debate would be the ones that must be fact.

The end result was something he was proud of, a masterpiece called *Diol-ogo sopra i due Massimi Sistemi del Mondo, Tolomaico e Copernico* (*Dialogue of Galileo Galilei on the Two Chief Systems of the World, the Ptolemaic and the Copernican*), com-pleted late in 1629. Galileo brought the manuscript to Rome with him in May of 1630 and showed it to Father Niccolo Riccardi, who was chief cen-sor of the press. The role of the chief censor was to examine books that were to be printed and make sure there was nothing unholy or illegal contained within them. If there were any problems with the text, the censor would tell the author which passages had to be changed or deleted in order for the manuscript to be published.

PUBLISHING·TROUBLES

CENSOR RICCARDI examined the book closely and made suggested changes to passages in which the Copernican theory seemed to get favorable treatment over the Ptolemaic system. Besides that, the book also needed a conclusion that was more favorable to the Ptolemaic system and a preface that explained the hypothetical nature of the arguments for the Copernican theory. It was acceptable to discuss the Copernican theory, but Galileo had to proclaim right at the start of the book that these were only ideas, not facts.

Galileo was not against these changes. The main thing for him was to see the work published. He later wrote: "I do not refuse to name these thoughts of mine with the title of chimeras, dreams, paralogisms [false arguments], and vain fantasies; entrusting and submitting the whole to the absolute knowledge and science of my Superiors."

Galileo also met with Pope Urban VIII while in Rome, who seemed friendly enough not to cause Galileo any alarm. Meanwhile, the summer sun began to warm up, and Galileo became uncomfortable in the heat of the Roman city. When Galileo returned to Florence in June 1630, he had permission from Riccardi to print the book in Rome. Riccardi still wished to see the book again before it was printed.

Galileo's original plan was that he would make the requested changes upon returning to Tuscany, and then send it to the learned Federico Cesi, who was the head of the Lincei Academy. To Galileo's shock and dismay, he

(RELATIVE MOTION) EXPERIMENT

GALILEO'S WORKS are full of examples and simple demonstrations. He uses these to build arguments or clarify points. While some are purely mathematical proofs, others use real objects to prove a point. In some cases, Galileo is trying to show that things that might be expected to act or appear to act one way in reality act another way. Galileo's genius was to go beneath the surface and examine something closely. In this experiment, Galileo was trying to make a point about the Copernican theory and the movement of the earth.

MATERIALS
* Large bowl (7 inches [18 cm] across)
* Water
* Small, hollow plastic ball (such as a ping-pong ball)
* Coffee scoop

Fill the bowl most of the way with water. Place the ball in the water. Hold the rim of the bowl tightly with both hands, one on each side. Now, turn the bowl to the right suddenly as if it is a steering wheel. Which direction does the ball move compared to the bowl?

Now, take the ball out and replace it with the empty coffee scoop. Imagine what would happen if you turned the bowl. Which direction do you think the coffee scoop would turn, based on what you observed in the first part of the experiment? Try it. Which direction does the coffee scoop actually move?

(**Hint:** *Keep an eye on the scoop handle as a reference point.*)

learned that on August 1 Cesi had died suddenly after a few days' illness. To make matters worse, an epidemic of the plague hit Florence during this time, and communication between Rome and Florence was difficult. The death of his powerful supporter, Cesi, seemed to change the political climate, and Galileo decided to seek a license to print the manuscript in Florence instead of Rome. He was given the go-ahead in September 1630.

But Galileo first had to write to the Roman censor with whom he had dealt in the spring. Riccardi was not pleased with the change of plans and still wanted to see the manuscript again. Galileo could not travel to Rome again, with the plague quickly spreading, so he was asked to send the manuscript. This was no simple task, and Galileo found that the postmaster could not help him. According to the grand duke's secretary, due to the outbreak of the plague, the large package would not get across the Tuscan border anytime soon; it was hard enough to get regular letters sent with any success.

The anxious Galileo did not like the delays. The book should have been printed already, but between the death of Cesi and the plague, at times Galileo felt the book might never be published. Already in his mid-sixties, Galileo was not sure how much longer he had to live. His next idea was to transmit only the preface and the revised ending of the book to Riccardi. Thinking that Riccardi would refuse if he asked directly, Galileo asked Francesco Niccolini, the Tuscan ambassador at Rome, if he or his wife could intercede on his behalf to their friend Riccardi.

Riccardi agreed, as long as Galileo could locate an appropriate, highly trusted person in Florence to read the entire manuscript and act as censor. Galileo selected Father Jacinto Stefani, and Riccardi approved the choice. Stefani read the manuscript and made some more changes before giving his approval.

This pleased Galileo, who felt that Stefani had revised the work with the "greatest care." In fact, Galileo was touched when he heard that Stefani was moved to tears when he saw how much reverence Galileo gave to the "Authority of the Superiors." With the preface and conclusion sent out for

✤ WHAT IS TRUTH?

A fact is a statement or piece of information that cannot be challenged because it can be backed up and proven. Still, facts can be examined from different angles and interpreted differently. A belief is a personal view of how something works, and it cannot be proven or disproved; your beliefs can remain the same even if you are confronted with evidence that shows you are wrong. A theory is an idea about how something works that may be based on both observations and facts. A theory may be proven true or may be discredited. Theories are often modified and updated as more facts come to light.

review, Galileo had done his part. As the weeks passed without word from Riccardi, Galileo grew upset. Had Riccardi gone back on his word? When would this book be published?

The Tuscan ambassador at Rome, Niccolini, again interceded on Galileo's behalf and spoke with Riccardi. Though it had seemed Riccardi originally agreed to have someone in Florence review the manuscript, suddenly this was not good enough anymore. How could Stefani possibly know what the pope might be offended by? Riccardi asked.

Galileo was outraged when he heard of these fresh delays. He wrote to a friend that it seemed his "affairs are floating on a vast and endless ocean." In March, Galileo wrote to the grand duke's secretary, Andrea Cioli, complaining of the delays and explaining his state of mind. Weeks and months ago, he explained, he had heard that Riccardi was going to send back the preface and the conclusion, accommodated entirely to his satisfaction. He went on:

> Nevertheless, this has not been the result. The book sits in a corner, my life is being consumed, and I am in continual suffering . . . take the matter into your own hands, and act as you think best, so that I can, while life still remains, see what result I may expect from all my long and heavy labors . . . And because his Highness [the grand duke of Tuscany] is most kindly anxious to know of my state of health, I ask you to tell him I would be reasonably well in body if the suffering of the spirit did not afflict me.

It was now May 1631, and the impatient Galileo was able to get Riccardi to allow the inquisitor at Florence, Clemente Egidio, to look over the entire book and give Galileo final permission to publish it. While Egidio had the body of the manuscript from Galileo, Riccardi took his time sending Egidio the preface and conclusion with his own comments. Many weeks passed before Egidio had in his hands the materials from Riccardi, along with instructions as to how to revise them, making sure that the preface and conclusion agreed.

❊ WAS GALILEO EVER WRONG?

Even a genius can be wrong sometimes. Galileo was brilliant, and his discoveries and theories were almost always right on the mark. In one case, however, Galileo was behind the times. His study of comets led him to believe that they were not actually physical matter, but simply a trick of the sun's light. His beliefs were actually closer to the Aristotelian views on comets than they were to the observations Tycho Brahe and Philipp Apian had made during the comet of 1577. Galileo published his observations in a book called *The Assayer* in 1623 (see page 96), in answer to a Jesuit priest with whom he had a disagreement on comets.

Title page of Galileo's book *Dialogue of the Two Chief Systems*.

THE BOOK WAS finally published in Florence in February 1632, when Galileo was 68 years old. Galileo immediately gave a copy to the grand duke of Tuscany, Ferdinand II de' Medici. His Tuscan friends and supporters thought the book was excellent. But even after all the delays to revise and soften the contents of the book, *Dialogue of the Two Chief Systems* still caused quite a commotion among Galileo's enemies in the Church. Galileo made special copies to be sent to his Roman friends, but due to the quarantine of the plague, it was not until May that copies of the book reached Rome. There, Galileo's old friend Benedetto Castelli read and immensely enjoyed the book. Soon after, eight more copies found their way to Rome, reaching Cardinal Antonio Barberini (who was Pope Urban VIII's nephew), Ambassador Niccolini, and the censor, Riccardi. As these copies made the rounds, those who had opposed Galileo became enraged. Action was taken rapidly.

In August 1632 booksellers' copies were suddenly seized, and Galileo's publisher was ordered by the Church to stop printing the book and to give up any copies it had on hand. The publisher replied that the supply of books had already been exhausted. The Holy Office must have been furious that they were too late to stop the book from being distributed.

Grand Duke Ferdinand II was upset at this sudden, unexpected problem. He had his secretary, Cioli, draft a letter (which Galileo himself may have helped compose) to the Tuscan ambassador at Rome asking for an explanation:

His Highness is astonished at the supreme degree to which a book that had been already been submitted by the author himself to the competent Roman authorities, a book that had been corrected, altered, and modified to conform to the wishes of the Superior authorities charged with deletions and additions . . . stamped at the same time from Rome and Florence with double permission, that the book is suspect now, after two years and that it is forbidden for the author or printer to publish . . . His Highness is perfectly certain that the author has nothing in sight except the good of the Holy Church . . . His Highness is persuaded that the warlike intentions against Signor Galileo are driven only by a hatred violent and jealous, directed rather against the person and author than against his book.

The problem was that Galileo's former friend Pope Urban VIII became convinced that the character Simplicio was meant to represent him. Galileo's enemies, probably urged on by Galileo's foes Horatio Grassi and Christoph Scheiner, had poisoned the pope's thoughts with the idea that he was being ridiculed. "Of course this is meant to be you. See how Galileo mocks you," they said. This infuriated the pope, especially since he had supported Galileo for so many years. In fact, Urban was mistaken: the character of Simplicio

❈ DIALOGUE OF THE TWO CHIEF SYSTEMS

The book that Galileo waited so long to have published was a passionate argument for the triumph of science over instinct and the "old teaching" of Aristotle. Using characters named Salviati, Sagredo (both based on real life people), and Simplicio (an invented character), Galileo staged a heated dialogue among the three players.

Giovanni Francesco Sagredo was an open-minded character who was seemingly neutral in belief at the start of the dialogues. He was based upon a real person, a Venetian friend and pupil of Galileo's by the same name. Filippo Salviati was a believer in the Copernican theory and was also based on a real person, a Florentine man who was a student of Galileo's. The third character was named Simplicio, and he was more of an old-fashioned Aristotelian type who believed in the Ptolemaic system.

They talked about the properties of earth, the moon, the planets, the sun, and the stars. The arguments his characters put forth were the same ones that Galileo had held for 30 years, ever since he converted to the Copernican theory. One reason Galileo got into serious trouble is that Simplicio's argument's seemed not to be given as much weight as those the Copernicans used.

Galileo knew he had to start with the simple and work to the complex, to make a chain of logical arguments leading to the inevitable truth about the earth's movement. The first step was to challenge the ancient notion that everything in the heavens was unmovable and unchanging.

Continued on next page . . .

Dialogue of the Two Chief Systems—continued

Galileo took on the subject logically, addressing every possible doubt and counterargument he had ever run across. Galileo made his characters come alive and argue with each other.

In one scene, Sagredo told the story of a doctor performing a dissection of a corpse, showing how all the nerves ran along the spine and to the brain—not to the heart, as the ancient Greek philosopher Aristotle thought. Well, pronounced the skeptic Simplicio, if it weren't for what Aristotle wrote, I would believe what I see in front of me!

In another scene, the old-fashioned and somewhat foolish Simplicio tells the more scientific-minded Salviati that the earth is dynamic, always changing with winds, rains, and storms, and with plants and animals living and dying. You can't see, insists Simplicio, any of these changes in celestial bodies. Nothing new happens in the skies and nothing old is changed.

Salviati asks: Then you must consider China and America to be celestial bodies, since you cannot see any changes there?

Simplicio says: That it is different, because China and America are too far away to observe any changes firsthand, but I have heard about them through others who have been there.

Galileo's telescope in use.

Ah! says Salviati: If these places are too far to observe any changes, then consider how far away the moon and planets are. Certainly no firsthand reports have come from the heavens as of yet! If you can't know what is changing or unchanging in America, how can you say anything definite about the planets? . . . Besides, what about the sunspots that have been observed, and the "new stars" of 1572 and 1604?

Simplicio replies: There is no proof that those new stars are heavenly bodies. And the sunspots may be illusions of the telescope [this was an actual argument given by several nonbelievers after Galileo invented the telescope] . . .

Later, Simplicio once again discusses how the earth is changeable and the celestial bodies are not.

Sagredo says: Is it possible that the huge heavenly bodies are there just to service the transient earth, that they serve no other purpose than to exist forever, never changing, for us, the mortal earth?

And so the argument continues . . .

was more likely a caricature of Pope Paul V, a man with little taste for science. But it was too late—the pope's mind was made up, and now Galileo had to pay.

In September 1632 Galileo was ordered by the Inquisition to appear at Rome. Niccolini went to meet with the pope to try to talk to him about the situation. He found Urban to be fairly single-minded in his opinions. When Galileo's old age and poor health were brought up, the pope shrugged it off and said Galileo brought it upon himself. If he must come to Rome slowly, so be it, the pope told Niccolini, "but he must come."

Urban acknowledged that Galileo had been his friend, and that they had had many friendly conversations and even eaten meals together, but added that the proceedings were in the "interest of religion and of faith."

Galileo, meanwhile, was unhappy about the turn of events. After waiting all that time for the publication of his work, the moment had finally come, and now there were further complications. He wrote to fellow mathematician Cesare Marsili about his feelings:

This persecution has become so relentless, it is conducted with such furor, that in the end, it is fifteen days, the Congregation of the Holy Office has notified me that I must come before them by the end of the month. This citation causes me much uneasiness: not that I do not hope to justify myself and clarify my innocence and my zeal for the good of the Holy Church; but my advanced age combined with my infirmities, the worries that a long voyage will cause me, made more distressing by the fear of the Plague, all make me apprehensive of surviving the journey.

Galileo stalled as much as he could. On December 17 he was examined by a team of three doctors, who issued a medical certificate attesting to his poor health. They wrote that they found his pulse to be irregular every three or four beats, that he had a weakness of stomach, the depression of someone who is a hypochondriac, a serious hernia that had injured his peritoneum (the membrane that surrounds the internal organs), and an assorted variety of pains of the body. In their medical opinion, he was a very sick man, and any change to his conditions could be a risk to his life.

Unfortunately for Galileo, the medical certificate did nothing to change anyone's mind. The pope issued an order to the Inquisition of Florence that explained that Galileo's "subterfuge [trickery] would not be tolerated" any longer. The Holy Office of Rome would send *their own* doctor to see Galileo, and decide once and for all about the state of his health. If he were found to be healthy enough to travel, he would be immediately taken prisoner in iron chains and brought directly to Rome.

This was the last straw. It seemed unavoidable that Galileo should go to Rome, and better that he do it under his own free will than as a prisoner who was already in defiance before his trial even started. On January 11 the grand duke's secretary wrote to Galileo:

> *It is with chagrin that I bring a new imperative order that you are summoned to leave immediately for Rome. His Highness took a real part in your affair. But, in the end, it is of total necessity that the Superior Authority is obeyed, and His Highness regrets to find it impossible to save you from this voyage. In order to let you do this conveniently, His Highness puts at your disposition one of his litters [a comfortable covered compartment] and his driver.*

The letter of the grand duke could not be clearer or more final. Galileo was to leave as soon as possible. While making preparations to leave, Galileo managed to dash off a few letters. He was clearly angry at his accusers. In one letter, he wrote: "Our reverend fathers the Jesuits, took great pain to demonstrate that my book is more abominable and more dangerous for the Holy Church than the writings of [Martin] Luther and [John] Calvin [a French Protestant Reformer]." In his letter, he recalled how he had already tried to show that the Holy Scriptures must be left out of any discussions of science. Galileo was also very confused about his situation. To begin with, he had written his book as a dialogue and been careful to represent opposing points of view. On top of that, he knew that he had done everything he had been asked to do before getting his book printed. So what was the problem?

Galileo reluctantly left the calm of his beloved Arcetri home on January 20, 1633, carried in the litter provided by the grand duke. The 150-mile (240-km) trip was long and difficult. The *tramontana* (a cold wind from the mountains) was especially bad that time of year. He passed through windy and bleak territory and was quarantined for 18 days before he was allowed to continue. The grand duke's litter was not allowed to cross the frontier because of the quarantine (in case it was infected with plague), and so the Tuscan ambassador at Rome, Niccolini, sent his own litter to meet Galileo at Ponte Centino and take him the rest of the way. He at last arrived in Rome on February 13.

By grace of the pope, Galileo was allowed to stay at the home of Niccolini. It was only because of Galileo's relationship to the grand duke of Tuscany that the pope felt obliged to make a special exception. No further word came from the Holy Office, except that Galileo had to remain in the ambassador's residence.

The ambassador treated Galileo very kindly. His first days in Rome gave him some hope. Though confined inside, he felt that the irritation against him was lessening every day and that the many accusations against him had been boiled down to one accusation; that he had disobeyed the 1616 order not to "hold, defend, or treach" the Copernican theory. "On this one I think I can prove my innocence completely," said Galileo.

The ambassador sat down with the pope on February 27 and asked that the trial be conducted speedily so that Galileo could return to Florence, but

The view Galileo might have seen as he approached Rome.

the pope's reply was one of indifference. The trial would come, he said, when it came, when the inquisitors were ready for him. The pope told Niccolini that Galileo should never have written his controversial book to begin with.

Days and weeks passed. Though unhappy to be in this position, Galileo was hopeful that the commotion would die down and he would be allowed to return home soon. He continued to believe, as he wrote on March 5 to Geri Bocchineri (his daughter-in-law's brother and secretary to the grand duke): "The accusations against me are losing their gravity and . . . already some have been completely averted because of their evident insignificance. . . . We must wait until in the end, truth will triumph over lies."

In March, Niccolini again tried to get the pope to excuse Galileo from his pending trial, but the pope refused. "May God have mercy on him," Urban told Niccolini. Ambassador Niccolini tried to argue Galileo's case, but this just made the pope angry. The pope said Galileo would have to wait to defend himself until the trial.

Meanwhile, Grand Duke Ferdinand II tried to make some impression by sending letters to all 10 cardinals on the Holy Congregation of the Inquisition. Most were not particularly impressed by the letters, but two cardinals, Guido Bentivoglio and Desiderio Scaglia, were somewhat moved. Galileo was very thankful to the grand duke for all his help, and wrote: "His Highness will receive the reward from God that the protectors of the innocent deserve."

Finally, on April 12, 1633, the accusers were ready to examine Galileo, who appeared before the vice-commissioner of the Holy Office and two other examiners to answer a few preliminary questions. He was asked about what happened in 1616 when he was in Rome. He replied that he was told the opinion of Copernicus was against

Vatican Gardens at the Belvedere Courtyard in Rome. Vatican City, where the Palace of the Inquisition is located, is a complex of grand buildings and beautiful gardens.

the Holy Scriptures, and therefore could not be taught or held as fact, but only as conjecture.

The inquisitor listened with great interest to Galileo, and then spoke. He informed the old scientist that the actual order that was recorded said that Galileo should not "hold, defend, nor teach the opinion in any way whatsoever." Galileo said he simply did not remember if the cardinal told him verbally these exact words. He did, however, hand over the brief letter that Cardinal Bellarmino wrote to him on May 26, 1616 (see page 95). In the letter, only the words "cannot be defended or held" were used. He told the inquisitor that he relied upon the certificate as the final word on the matter, and kept it to remind himself of the restrictions placed upon him. Then came a critical question. The inquisitor asked Galileo whether, when asking permission to print his book, he told the master of the palace (the censor, Riccardi) about the command that had been issued to him.

Galileo replied that he did not think it was necessary to do so because his book was not in violation of the order. It was a dialogue about the two different proposed systems, and did not prove the Copernican theory, instead exposing its flaws. With that, the interview was over, and Galileo returned to the three spacious rooms that he had been given as lodgings. When he needed to stretch he could walk up and down the hallway in the building, but he could not go outside.

On April 25 Galileo was sick in bed and wrote to Bocchineri: "I have always hoped and I hope now more than ever, that my innocence and my sincerity are proved. It is becoming painful to write, and I will stop now." A couple of days later, Galileo was visited by one of the inquisitors, Father Vincenzo Maculano da Firenzuola. The purpose of his visit was to make Galileo openly admit that he had defended the Copernican theory, so that things might go better for him.

Meanwhile, a panel of three theological experts had looked over the evidence and come to some conclusions about the case. The experts, Agostino Oreggi, Melchior Inchofer, and Zaccharia Pasqualigo, seemed to agree on a few key points. One was that it seemed Galileo not only taught and discussed the Copernican theory, but also believed it not to be only a theory, but a truth. His arguments, the panel said, were a little too conclusive and persuasive to be strictly hypothetical. And, most importantly, the panel thought that Galileo had most certainly gone against the order given to him in 1616.

On April 30 Galileo was called back for a second interview. This time he was much more apologetic. He explained that he had gone through the book for the first time in a couple of years. He conceded that yes, it was possible in certain places in the book, a reader could possibly get the wrong impression. The arguments he put forth in favor of the Copernican theory—the sunspots and the existence of tides—"come to the ear of the reader with far greater force and power than should have been imparted to them by someone who regarded them [the theories] as inconclusive."

To this thought, Galileo added that if he were given the chance, he could demonstrate more strongly that the Copernican theory was false. He said: "I promise to criticize one by one the favorable arguments for the false and condemned opinion and I will refute them in the most solid manner of which God will inspire me. In consequence, I beg the high tribunal to help me in this good resolution and enable me to realize it as possible."

To his surprise, Galileo was allowed to return to the household of Ambassador Niccolini. He accepted an invitation from the archbishop of Siena, Ascanio Piccolomini, to stop there on his way home and wait out the last throes of the plague.

"The knowledge I have of the slowness of the heart of Rome makes me understand the lateness with which I will have the honor of your presence in this house," wrote Piccolomini to Galileo.

On May 10 Galileo was told he could prepare a defense and present it to the tribunal for their consideration. Once again, he referred to the certificate he had received from Cardinal Bellarmino in May 1616, which said he was only told not to hold or defend the Copernican theory. He told them that because he had the actual certificate, he thought nothing more about the verbal order of February 1616, and that the phrases "nor to teach it" and "in any way whatsoever" were not familiar in his memory. At the end of his statement of defense, he appealed to the mercy of the judges and reminded them that this whole affair had robbed him of his health and future:

Pray you take into consideration my pitiable state of physical indisposition, to which, at the age of seventy years, I have been reduced by ten months of constant mental anxiety and the fatigue of a long and difficult journey at the most inclement season, together with the loss of the greater part of the years of which, from my previous state of health, I had the prospect.

On June 21 Galileo again appeared before the judges. They asked him very pointedly: did he ever hold the Copernican theory? Galileo must have sensed the importance of his answer, because he was quite cautious. He told them he used to be indifferent to either system before 1616, but that after he was "assured of the wisdom of the authorities," he believed in the Ptolemaic system. The judges did not believe this answer. They told him that by virtue of having written *Dialogue of the Two Chief Systems,* Galileo did hold the prohibited opinion.

Galileo insisted this was not the case: "My object being to make it clear that neither one set of arguments nor the other has the force of conclusive demonstration in favor of this opinion or that opinion . . . I affirm, therefore, on my conscience, that I do not now hold the condemned opinion, and have not held it since the decision of the authorities." The judges now decided to use intimidation, and they threatened Galileo with torture. In a document of June 16, the Holy Congregation stated: "The Holy Congregation decrees Galileo will be interrogated concerning his intentions and threatened with torture." Frightened, Galileo reaffirmed that he had not held the opinion since he was forbidden to in 1616. That was the end of the trial of Galileo.

Тне morning of June 22, 1633, Galileo was taken to the beautiful gothic-style building that housed the convent of St. Maria. He was wearing the white robe of a penitent, someone who has sinned. As Galileo knelt before them, a stern voice slowly read the opinion of the cardinals:

[As] you Galileo, son of the late Vincenzo Galileo of Florence, now . . . age seventy, were denounced in 1615 by the Holy Office, that you held as the truth the false doctrine taught by many, that the sun is the center of the world and immovable, and that the earth moves . . .

Seeing that you had numerous disciples, to whom you taught this same doctrine: That you maintained a correspondence with some German mathematicians; also that you published letters on the Sunspots, in which you set forth this doctrine as true; and that to the objections put forward from Holy Scriptures, you replied by interpreting it according to your own ideas. And following this was presented a copy of a [letter], that was said to have been written by you . . . in which following the position of Copernicus, are contained various propositions against the true sense and authority of the Holy Scriptures.

This Holy Tribunal, wishing to act upon the disorder and the damage that have resulted . . . and which was constantly growing to the prejudice of the Holy Faith; by the order of our Lord Pope . . . the two propositions of the stability of the sun and the motion of the earth were judged by qualified theologians as follows:

That the sun is the center of the universe and does not move from its place is a notion that is absurd and false in philosophy, and heretical; being expressly contrary to Holy Writings. That the earth is not the center of the universe nor immovable, but that it moves, and also rotates, is likewise a proposition absurd and false in philosophy, and considered . . . to be erroneous in faith.

But willing at the time to proceed kindly toward you, it was decreed in the Sacred Congregation held before our Lord Pope on the 25th of February 1616: That the most

Eminent Lord Cardinal Bellarmino order you [to] entirely leave and reject this false doctrine . . . that you were not to teach it to other people, nor to hold or defend it, [and] if you did not acquiesce [give in], you were to be incarcerated; and in the execution of the said decree, the following day . . . after having been gently advised and admonished by the said Lord Cardinal, you . . . receive[d] a precept [order] . . . that you should entirely abandon the stated false opinion, and . . . neither uphold nor teach it in any way whatsoever, not orally, not in writing, and having promised to obey, you were allowed to leave.

And so that this pernicious [stubborn] doctrine might be rooted out and prevented from spreading . . . a decree was issued from the Holy Congregation of the Index, prohibiting those books, that treated said doctrine, which was declared false, and entirely contrary to the sacred and divine Scriptures.

And there having lately appeared a book published in Florence [last] year . . . the title being: Dialogue of Galileo Galilei on the Two Chief Systems of the World, the Ptolemaic and the Copernican. *And the Sacred Congregation having been informed that in consequence of the said book the false opinion of the movement of the earth and the stability of the sun was daily gaining ground, the said book was diligently considered, and was found to openly transgress [go against] the precept that had been made to you, [because] you . . . defended the already condemned opinion, which had been declared false in front of your face; whereas in the book you [use various] tricks . . . to persuade yourself that you leave it undecided and merely probable. This however is a most serious error, since in no way can an opinion be probable that has been declared and defined to be contrary to Holy Scripture.*

Wherefore by Our order you were . . . examined under oath, you acknowledged to have written and had published the said book. You confessed that about ten or twelve years ago, after having received the precept mentioned above, you started to

Galileo before the Inquisition.

write the book. That you asked for a license to print the book without signifying that . . . you had a precept not to hold, defend, or teach in any way at all the doctrine.

You also confessed that the writings of said book, in many passages, lead the reader to form the idea that the arguments . . . in favor of the false opinion, were more likely to convince than . . . to overturn . . .

And a convenient time having been assigned for your defense, you produced a certificate written [by] the most eminent Signor Cardinal Bellarmino that you [obtained] . . . to defend against the calumnies of your enemies, who said on the contrary that you abjured and were punished by the Holy Office. In that certificate it says, that you have not abjured nor been punished, but that only the declaration made by our Pope and published by the sacred Congregation of the Index, had been announced to you, in which it is declared that the doctrine of the motion of the earth and the stability of the sun is contrary to the Sacred Scriptures and therefore cannot be defended or held. And seeing as in this certificate there is no mention of . . . the order not "to teach" and "in any way," you represented that we should believe that in the course of fourteen or sixteen years you had lost all memory of them; and this was why you said nothing about the [order] when you asked permission to print your book . . . .

But this document, produced for your defense, aggravates your position, since it declares the aforesaid opinion contrary to Holy Scriptures, and shows that, nevertheless, you have dared to expound it, and to represent it as probable.

You cannot, furthermore, be exonerated [cleared from blame] by a printing license which you obtained by artful and cunning means, and by hiding the order that had been imposed on you. And [because] you [did not speak] the truth as to your intentions, we have deemed it necessary to resort to a rigorous personal examination, in which . . . you have answered like a good Catholic. Therefore . . . we have arrived at this final sentence against you:

. . . we say, pronounce, sentence, declare that you . . . have rendered yourself strongly suspect of heresy by the Holy Office, in that you believed and maintained a doctrine that is erroneous and contrary to the Holy and Divine Scriptures, namely: that the sun is the center of the world, that it does not move from east to

west, that the earth moves, and is not the center of the universe . . . and consequently you incur all the censures and penalties enacted and [proclaimed] in the sacred canons . . . from which penalties it pleases us to absolve you on the condition that, with a sincere heart, and without any concealment or reservation, you, in our presence, abjure, cease, and abhor the abovementioned heresies and errors, and all other heresies and errors contrary to the Catholic, Apostolic, and Roman Church, according to the formula we impose on you:

And to the end that your pernicious error and grave sin may not remain unpunished, and to the end that in the future you might be more cautious, and may serve as an example to others, we order that by public edict the book Dialogues of Galileo Galilei *is prohibited [banned].*

We condemn you to the special prison of our Holy Office for a time to be decided later, and by way of salutary penance, we require that for three years once a week you recite the seven Penitential Psalms.

We reserve the right of diminishing, modifying, or lifting in its entirety the abovementioned penalties and penance. . . .

Galileo listened as the cardinals told him they thought he had tried to trick them, pretending to leave the subject of the two systems open for the reader to decide. He heard with great distress the wrath he had inspired in Rome. The speech he had just heard was certainly long and detailed. The cardinals seemed to have a great deal of anger over his book. It seemed almost unreal, listening to his life being put on hold for a scientific book he wrote. After all, his intention had never been to bring the Church into any of this. It was not a religious book, and it made no reference to the Church or the pope. But they said it very plainly: they wished to make an example of him.

What was this imprisonment they spoke of? This had not even seemed possible a few days earlier. He thought he would be on his way back home, cleared of any wrongdoing. But before he could let his thoughts go any further, he had to do as he was told and apologize and recant his beliefs.

With the passage of time after Galileo's death, rumors spread about him being imprisoned in Rome and being tortured. This never happened. Some said that Galileo had been imprisoned in the jail of the Inquisition for weeks, but in fact he was comfortably housed in an ordinary apartment for a matter of days before returning to the Tuscan ambassador's home. Another myth was that Galileo was blinded by the inquisitors.

It was also a common myth that, after he was forced to recant his beliefs before the tribunal, he muttered under his breath: *"E pur si muove"* ("And yet it moves"). There is little probability that he ever said this: this particular legend was only begun after his death.

❧ THE·ABJURATION·OF·GALILEO ❧

FOLLOWING THE reading of the sentence, Galileo was made to read a statement of apology and abjuration (meaning he took back what he said) that had been prepared for him. He had to kneel and read it in front of the assembled members of the Inquisition in order to escape more serious punishment. With his voice trembling, he said

I, Galileo Galilei, son of the late Vincenzio Galilei of Florence, seventy years old, tried personally by this court, and kneeling before You, the most Eminent and Reverend Lord Cardinals, Inquisitors-General throughout the Christian Republic against heretical depravity, having before my eyes the Most Holy Gospels, and laying on them my own hands; I swear that I have always believed, I believe now, and with God's help I will in future believe all which the Holy Catholic and Apostolic Church do hold, preach, and teach. But since I, after having been admonished by this Holy Office entirely to abandon the false opinion that the sun was the center of the universe and immovable, and that the earth was not the center of the same and that it moved, and that I was neither to hold, defend, or teach in any way whatsoever, either orally or in writing, the stated false doctrine and after having received a notification that the said doctrine is contrary to the Holy Writings, I did write and cause to be printed a book in which I treat of the said already condemned doctrine, and bring forth arguments of much [effectiveness] in its favor, without arriving at any solution: I have been judged vehemently suspected of heresy, that is, of having held and believed that the sun is the center of the universe and immovable, and that the earth is not the center of the same, and that it does move.

Consequently, wishing to erase from the minds of your Eminences and all faithful Christians this vehement suspicion rightly conceived against me, I abjure with a sincere heart and without mental reservation, I curse and detest the said errors and heresies, and generally all and every error and sect contrary to the Holy Catholic

Church. And I swear that for the future I will neither say nor affirm in speech or writing such things as might bring upon me similar suspicion and if I know any heretic, or one suspected of heresy, I will denounce him to this Holy Office, or to the Inquisitor and Ordinary of the place in which I may be living. I furthermore swear and promise to adopt and observe entirely all the punishments which have been or may be imposed on me by this Holy Office. And if I go against any of these said promises, protests, or oaths (this God should not wish) I submit myself to all the pains and penalties which by the Sacred Canons and other Decrees general and particular are against such offenders imposed and promulgated. So help me God and the Holy Evangel, which I touch with my own hands.

I Galileo Galilei have abjured, sworn, and promised, and hold myself bound as above; and in token of the truth, with my own hand have subscribed the present schedule of my abjuration, and have recited it word by word. In Rome, at the Convent della Minerva, the 22nd day of June, 1633.

SERVING·THE·SENTENCE

THE CONDEMNATION and humiliation of both Galileo and his theories seemed enough to please Urban VIII. He decided Galileo would not actually be imprisoned in any kind of jail or dungeon. The first place Galileo was sent for his punishment was the grand duke of Tuscany's villa near Rome; but Galileo did not wish to remain anywhere near Rome. He got up the nerve to write a letter to Pope Urban VIII asking for a favor:

Galileo Galilei begs humbly your Holiness to assign a different residence that could be given him as a prison. Your Holiness can choose himself the place in Florence he judges convenient. Two reasons cause Galileo to address this demand. The first is the bad state of his health, and the second is that the suppliant [Galileo] expects his sister who arrives from Germany with eight children [his younger brother Michelangelo had died in Germany in 1631, leaving a wife and children behind], and only he can offer them hospitality. He will be thankful for any decision your Holiness makes.

The pope's main objective was to see that Galileo was shut away from the world. It did not matter so much where this occurred. Though Galileo wished to return to the Florence area, it was decided instead that he was to go to Siena, which is 35 miles (55 km) south of Florence. There, he would stay at the grand home of his powerful friend Ascanio Piccolomini. Since 1628 Piccolomini had been the archbishop of Siena. The archbishop had, since his youth, admired Galileo. On July 6 Galileo began the trip and felt well enough to walk 4 miles (6 km) by foot. Galileo arrived at Siena on July 9, 1633, and he was received with warmth and admiration by Piccolomini.

"Today I write to you, pressed by the boredom of a captivity that has already lasted six months, captivity rendered more distressing by the chagrin and worries of the preceding year . . . I was sent to this archbishop's palace, where for the last fifteen days I am complimented by the [inexpressible] kindness of the excellent Monsignor the Archbishop," he wrote to Cioli on July 27.

During this time, Galileo took the opportunity to do some scientific work, when his health permitted. A young Florentine man, upon recommendation of one of Galileo's friends, sent some mathematical problems. Galileo was happy to have something to "give my thoughts an entirely different direction," and the fact that his friends still regarded him highly "makes my chagrin seem less heavy." Still, he could not help but think every day how he was still there against his will. Under the Church's ruling, he was not allowed to leave the archbishop's palace and accompany Piccolomini to a summer villa.

❋ THE PICCOLOMINI FAMILY

The Archbishop Ascanio Piccolomini (1597-1671) came from an old and respected Siena family. His family tree included two popes (Pius II [1405-1464] and Pius III [1439-1503]), a general in the imperial army named Ottavio Piccolomini (1599-1656), as well as Alessandro Piccolomini (1508-1578), who was a writer, philosopher, and astronomer who had published a celestial atlas in 1540. There were also numerous barons, dukes, counts, and princes in the family. The archbishop embraced Galileo's theories and was a gracious host while Galileo was in Siena for five months.

Another member of the same illustrious family whom Galileo knew was Enea Silvio Piccolomini (who lived in Florence at the time), who was a general in the army of the grand duke of Tuscany.

Galileo's daughter wrote about the affairs of the Galilei property back at Arcetri, and this only made Galileo long more strongly for a return to Florence. She told him of the lemons, oranges, and plums ripening in the garden, the beans that were waiting to be picked, and the pigeons that were ready to be eaten. She lamented Galileo's separation from Arcetri and wondered if there was anything she could do to get him released from his Siena imprisonment. Maria Celeste got a hold of a copy of her father's official sentence, and even began to say for her father the Penitential Psalms that were a part of the punishment.

Every morning, aching and old, Galileo woke up and realized he was in someone else's house. It was a sad feeling. He asked Niccolini to request a transfer back to Arcetri, but was rejected. Niccolini knew the whole trial was too fresh in the pope's mind and asking too soon would be of no use. Galileo remained where he was for five long months. By December he seemed to be losing hope: "I await a decision from Rome, but I do not hold out hope that it will be favorable," he wrote.

At last, that same month, he was given permission to move back to his villa at Arcetri. Called Giojello, the villa was located just 1 mile (1.5 km) from Florence. By this time, the plague had finally receded from Florence, and so it was safe to go back. Galileo's villa was located on a hill with a pretty orchard and vineyard. The building itself had a "tower" where Galileo could observe the night skies with his telescope. He was not supposed to have many visitors at once, and was to pass his days in quiet retirement there, according to the pope. How glad he was to be home! Soon after arriving, he wrote how good it was to "breathe this healthful air of my dear homeland Florence."

View of Siena in the 19th century. The cathedral and adjacent palace where Galileo resided are seen at the top right of the picture.

MARIA CELESTE's health was very poor. The extreme conditions in the convent did not help. Such conditions could turn a sniffle into a serious ailment, a cough into a deathly illness. Toward the end of 1633, Maria Celeste tried to prepare her father for her impending death. Things did not improve, and at the end of March 1634, she suffered from a devastating illness called dysentery and died on April 1 at the age of 34.

Galileo's grief was severe. The blow of being sentenced to house arrest was one thing, but now the loss of his beloved daughter at such a young age was almost too much to bear. He blamed her death in part on her sadness at his being away for so long, which led her health to deteriorate considerably. He wrote to a friend that he heard his daughter calling to him from heaven, and believed he had not the strength or health to live much longer.

Galileo later wrote to a friend about the circumstances of his daughter's death:

> During my absence, believing me in grave danger, she had fallen into a profound melancholy that had destroyed her health; she was in the end seized by a violent dysentery such that in six days she left this earth. I remain prey to an unspeakable chagrin, aggravated still more by the following circumstance:
>
> I came back from the convent to the house [after visiting her when she was very sick in March], accompanied by the doctor who had cared for my daughter. He had warned me that he did not have much hope that she would last through the next day. Arriving at my villa, I found the vicar of the Inquisition who communicated to me the order of the Holy Office, coming from Rome, with a letter from Cardinal Barberini . . .

Because Galileo's health was only getting worse, he had asked his trusted ally Niccolini, the Tuscan ambassador, to get permission from the pope to move into the actual city of Florence, so he could receive the proper medical care his condition required. The request was soundly rejected in the

(PROJECTILE MOTION EXPERIMENT)

GALILEO WAS very interested in problems relating to the military, including fortifications and also the motion of projectiles. In this activity, you will try to observe one theory that Galileo proved, that projectiles travel through the air in the path of a parabola, or open curve.

MATERIALS

* Open field or playground
* Tennis ball or small rubber ball
* A friend
* Notebook
* Pen

Go to an open field or playground. Pick the direction you will throw the projectile (your ball), and have your friend stand at about a 45-degree angle to the path the ball will be thrown, about 40 feet (12 m) away from you. Now, throw the tennis ball into the air as hard and far as you can, aiming about 3 to 4 feet (about 1 m) above your head. Have your friend observe and chart the projectile's path as it goes up, and its path as it descends back down toward the ground.

Now, have your friend move closer to you, still on a diagonal to the path of the ball. This time, aim the ball at an imaginary point about 10 feet (3 m) or so above your head and about 15 feet (4.5 m) in front of you. Have your friend again observe and chart the path (also known as trajectory) of the ball. A tennis ball moves relatively slowly compared to a cannonball bursting from a cannon or a bullet whizzing out of the barrel of a gun, so it is much easier to observe. Though these "real" pro-

jectiles travel faster and farther than an ordinary ball might travel, they still observe the same laws.

Catapults, projectile firing systems used since ancient times, relied upon the "arc" effect that a projectile displayed when fired a long distance into the air. Those who operated catapults had to determine where to set up their equipment to get the best shot at their targets.

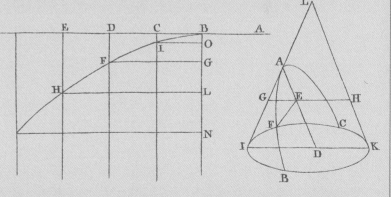

Mathematical drawings from Galileo's work on the parabolic movement of a projectile.

letter from the cardinal that he found waiting for him at his villa that March day.

In fact, Cardinal Barberini told Galileo not to even ask such things any more. Galileo wrote, "I must abstain in the future from asking permission to return to Florence, or they would take me back [to Rome], and put me into the actual prison of the Holy Office."

ENEMIES·STILL·ABOUND

GALILEO WAS convinced that his enemies were still at work trying to make his life more difficult. He spoke of the "vigilant activity" that his enemies were undertaking against him. One example Galileo was angry about in 1634 was when a letter that had been addressed to him was intercepted and delivered to Cardinal Barberini. Luckily, the letter's contents were not damaging to Galileo. Another example was a report he heard from one of his close friends who had been speaking with Father Christopher Grienberger, mathematician in the Collegio Romano (Roman College). Grienberger said that if Galileo had only remained in the good graces of the Jesuit fathers at the college, nothing bad would have happened to him, and he could have written what he wanted, even on the movement of the earth.

Galileo said about this incident: "It is not for this or that opinion that I have been persecuted, but because I have incurred the disgrace of the Jesuits." Further annoying to Galileo, another Jesuit father from Vienna named Melchior Inchofer had published in Rome the opinion that the movement of the earth was the most scandalous and wicked of all the heresies. Inchofer had been one of the theologians on the panel that had examined Galileo's book for the Inquisition. As Galileo wrote in a letter to his friend Elia Diodati in July 1634:

[Inchofer wrote] that one can tolerate in academic professorships, in public discussions, and in printed works all the arguments against the principal articles of faith, against immortality of the spirit, against creation, against incarnation, etc., with the sole exception of the dogma relative to the immobility of the earth . . . this article of faith is considered so [sacred] before all others that it is not [allowable] to express in a discussion any argument against it.

Work seemed to rescue Galileo from the worst despair. It occupied his mind and gave him a reason to live. Or to put it another way, he figured he shouldn't waste time while he was still alive, so he chose to work hard. His mind was still ripe with fresh ideas. *Dialogue of the Two Chief Systems* was not his last work. He set about other projects and experiments to the extent that his health allowed.

And though the Catholic Church had condemned him, his reputation around the world as a man of brilliant intellect still drew him attention. The year before she died, Maria Celeste had written to him to reassure him that he had not lost any stature: "If for a brief moment your name and fame were clouded, they are now restored to greater brightness than ever."

The attention he got from friends and others during his seclusion seemed to prove she was right. In 1634 he received an English visitor, a philosopher who was touring Europe. This man was named Thomas Hobbes. The young Hobbes was so impressed by his discussions with Galileo that he later incorporated some of Galileo's ideas into his philosophical works. He believed that human life is governed strictly by peoples' movement—through space (geometry and physics) and in relation to one another (ethics and politics). Hobbes was best known for a philosophical work about government called *The Leviathan,* published in 1651

Although Galileo was depressed about his sentence and his deteriorating health, in his heart he knew he had not disrespected any true Christian teachings and had not truly harmed the Church. He felt his conscience was clear and he was innocent, and that gave him comfort.

Thomas Hobbes was influenced by his meeting with Galileo.

7

GALILEO'S LAST DAYS

"I find myself in bed for five weeks, exhausted of my strength," Galileo wrote to his friend and patron Elia Diodati on July 4, 1637. He further wrote: "In addition, more sorrow, the total loss of my right eye . . . and the other eye, already imperfect, is of little use due to a profusion [great quantity] of tears."

Already blind in one eye, Galileo looked at his reflection. Staring back at him was an old man with a heavily creased forehead, slightly sunken cheeks, receding gray hair, and a heavy gray beard. It was 1638, and Galileo was now 74. Many acquaintances and friends he had known from his days at the university were already long dead. Johannes Kepler had died in 1630, as had his close friend and supporter Federico Cesi. Others had followed, including his beloved daughter Maria Celeste in 1634. The days passed, as always, but were not full with promise as they had once been.

HIS·LAST·WORK

Now, nearing total blindness, Galileo realized the irony of his situation. The very eyes that had seen deep into the heavens, that had peered countless hours into his telescope, were now about to fail him forever. No more would he study the sun and the planets. It would be a never-ending nighttime, but one with no moon and no stars, only darkness.

He again wrote to his friend Diodati about the hopelessness of the situation: "This heaven, this earth, this universe, that I, by my marvelous discoveries and clear demonstrations had enlarged a hundred thousand times beyond the belief of the wise men of bygone ages, from now on is shrunk into the small space filled only by my bodily sensations."

For all of his work in optics, all the lenses he had studied to magnify and draw in light, none of that could help him to see again. Though he held out hope for a while that his eyesight might be regained, eventually he resigned himself to the fact that he was blind and would remain so for the rest of his life.

Just a few weeks before he lost his remaining eyesight, Galileo had completed his last studies of the heavens, finding proof that the earth's moon "librated," or wobbled slightly, on its axis in relation to the earth. Yes, there was so much more to discover in the skies. Others, however, would have to continue his work.

He was very glad, though, that he managed to finish his last manuscript, *Discorsi e dimostrazioni matematiche intorno a due nove Scienze* (*Discourses and Mathematical Demonstrations of Two New Sciences*), before he could not see any longer. This last work he considered his masterpiece, even better than the work that had left him a prisoner in his own house. He dedicated the book to the kind Count François de Noailles, who was the ambassador to France at Rome and a former student of his at Padua.

Still, under the rules of his sentence, he could not publish it in Italy. Thankfully, the manuscript for *Two New Sciences* was smuggled out of Italy and would be published in Amsterdam, Holland, in 1638. Galileo realized he would not have the pleasure of paging through the finished book because of his failing sight. *If God has taken my vision, so be it*, he thought, but it would not stop him from using his mind and imagination to continue in whatever scientific work he could manage in the time he had left.

HIS·BEST·WORK

I N *Two New Sciences,* Galileo dealt with issues of physics that did not have to do with astronomy. The new manuscript was another dialogue among the same three characters that had got him into so much trouble six years before: Sagredo, Salviati, and Simplicio. Full of math and physics, the new book contained nothing very controversial to the Church. Still, it was daring for him to have used Simplicio again, with Pope Urban VIII still in power.

The book's dialogues take place over the course of four days. Day one's discussion deals with the resistance solid bodies offered against fracture. The second day is devoted to the cause of cohesion (molecules adhering to

---

✸ THE LIFE OF GALILEO: A PLAY

Bertolt Brecht (1898–1956) was a German writer who completed a play called *Leben des Galilei* (*The Life of Galileo*) in 1947. He is best known for his musical play *Die Dreigroschenoper* (*The Threepenny Opera*) of 1928.

In *The Life of Galileo*, there are more than 50 characters, including Cosimo II de' Medici, Galileo's daughter Virginia (Maria Celeste), the doge of Venice, and three cardinals. Though it covers most of his life, the play focuses on Galileo's astronomical discoveries and the Inquisition that resulted from the publication of his discoveries. The play ends with the manuscript for his last work, *Two New Sciences*, being smuggled across the Italian border.

In the first American performance of the play, the actor Charles Laughton (famous for his role in the film *Mutiny on the Bounty*) played Galileo.

(ACCELERATED MOTION)

AMONG THE TOPICS that interested Galileo for many years was the accelerated motion of bodies. When a body falls through the air, it does not travel at a uniform speed. Its velocity (speed) increases the farther it falls. In this activity, you will observe this idea.

MATERIALS

* Small wooden stake (less than 2 feet [60 cm] long)
* Ruler (12-inch [30-cm])
* Brick (from a garden or home supply store)
* Pencil
* Notebook

Go outdoors and find a spot where the ground is not too rocky. Insert the stake into the ground just enough so it stands up by itself. Measure how much of the stake remains above the ground. Hold the brick so it is 1 inch (2.5 cm) above the stake. Now, drop the brick. Does the stake move into the ground any farther? Measure how much of the stake remains above ground. Using your pencil, record this in your notebook. Now, replace the stake in a different spot so that it is back to the original depth. Hold the brick 3 inches (7.5 cm) directly above the stake and let go. Record how many inches the stake has been driven into the ground. Repeat again, replacing the stake and holding the brick 6 inches (15 cm) above the stake. Be careful not to let the brick hit your toes! Try again with the brick 1 foot (30.5 cm) above the stake, and then 2 feet (0.5 m) above.

Galileo was trying to show that the force of an object is not due to its weight alone, but also to its speed. Further, he wanted to illustrate that the speed of an object is not uniform, but increases as it falls. An object falling from a great distance has a much greater force than the same object falling from a lesser distance. Therefore, the amount that the stake is driven into the ground when the brick is 6 inches (15 cm) above it will not be six times the amount the stake moves when the brick is 1 inch (2.5 cm) above it. Rather, it will be more than six times the distance.

one another). The third day discusses uniform motion (constant speed) and naturally accelerated motion (increasing speed), and the fourth day covers the topic of violent motions and projectiles.

Even in his old age, Galileo was determined to uncover the truth about many questions of physics. He made observations that would be very useful to engineers and architects of the future. The strength of materials was of interest to Galileo. He noted that there is a physical difficulty of building anything extremely large—including ships, palaces, or churches. Nature cannot create trees larger than a certain size, or their branches would break off under the strain of their own weight.

He discovered that a beam of a certain length and width has the ability to carry a load of a certain amount before beginning to break. In one illustration from his work, a wooden beam is shown coming out of a stone wall, with a hook on the end from which a weight is suspended. If that beam were doubled in length and width, the amount of weight it could support would not be double. Rather, Galileo showed that the width of the beam had to be increased by a larger factor if the length were doubled.

This brought Galileo to the topic of animals. If this principle was true for a wooden beam, it was also true for a bone. The wooden beam was in effect the skeleton of a ship or a house. Galileo wrote that the larger an animal's size, the more substantial in size its bones have to be to bear the weight. While a smaller animal such as a dog could carry twice its weight, perhaps managing to support another dog on its back, a large animal such as a horse or elephant could not support one of its own kind without being severely injured.

The laws of physics meant that trees and animals could only reach a certain size before they would collapse under the immense pressure of their own weight. This principle explains why very tall people have more back trouble than shorter people; their bones are not built to support the weight as well. Nature was subject to certain restrictions under the laws of physics. Engineers use this principle when designing buildings and bridges. A suspension bridge, for example, uses a long deck that is supported (or suspended) by cables.

Illustration from *Two New Sciences* showing a beam extending from a stone wall.

SICK·BUT·STILL·BUSY

I N EARLY 1638 an inquisitor named Fanano visited Galileo to see his living conditions and the state of his health. The inquisitor found a broken man. Galileo was completely blind, suffering from a hernia, various bodily pains, and severe insomnia. Fanano described Galileo as looking more like a corpse than a living man.

At this point, the number of Galileo's visitors was reduced, and Galileo's now-attentive son was instructed not to let visitors stay for too long, so as not to overtire his father. In the spring of 1638, Galileo miraculously received

Ratio of bone width to length means that an elephant's relative strength is less than that of a smaller animal.

permission from the pope to go into the city of Florence and receive medical treatment. He was warned, even though he was 74 years old and very frail, that he was not to go out and about the city streets of Florence, and not to talk to anyone at all about the Copernican theory that had been condemned.

Around this time, Galileo heard back about an offer he had made to the government of Holland. Two years before, he had offered them his method of finding longitude using the position of Jupiter's moons. He had hinted that he also had invented a way to use the pendulum in a clock in order to make

(BEAM STRENGTH GAME)

GALILEO DEMONSTRATED that the strength of a piece of a certain material depends on its size and shape, and also how the weight is carried. In this activity, you will try to prove that this is true.

MATERIALS
* Wooden ruler

A standard wooden ruler is 12 inches (30.5 cm) long, about 1 inch (2.5 cm) wide, and about 1/8 inch (0.3 cm) thick. Galileo showed in his book *Two New Sciences* that the same beam has more strength when held in one direction than in the other direction. Hold the ruler with a thumb and forefinger at each end so the numbers are parallel to the ground. Try to bend the ruler. Does it bend easily? Now, hold the ruler so that the numbers are facing you, with your thumb and forefinger on the top and bottom of each end. Try to bend the ruler. Does it bend easily? Which way do you think the ruler would be able to hold more weight?

If you were to embed the ruler into a stone wall both ways, the ruler would bear more weight standing on end because it has greater resistance along the longer distance of the fulcrum, or stationary point to which the force is being applied. When holding the ruler on end, the fulcrum is along the line that

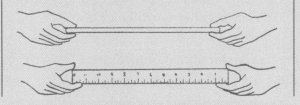

measures about 1 inch (2.5 cm). When holding the ruler the other way, the fulcrum is on a line that measures just a fraction of an inch. The strength of the ruler when held the second way is very minimal. It also makes a difference where the weight is suspended from.

Try holding the ruler flat and bending it again. Now, move one hand to the middle of the ruler and bend. Move your thumb and forefinger closer to the end your other hand is holding. The strength of the ruler and ability to withstand weight is increased as you get closer to the fulcrum.

This property of materials is why buildings, bridges, and other structures have vertical columns supporting the horizontal beams; the strength of beams is most effective at a certain length.

it more accurate. Many years had passed since the original negotiations with the government of Spain, and now Galileo was just hoping he could get someone to accept his idea as being useful. In fact, he did not even request any payment. Perhaps it bothered him that this technology was still lying unused in his possession.

The government of Holland took their time discussing and debating the merits and practicalities of Galileo's method. They appointed a commission of four men to examine the technology, including two mathematicians and a geographer. The commission debated and then finally in August of 1638 sent two brothers from Holland to visit Galileo at his villa at Arcetri.

They brought with them a letter of thanks from the government of Holland and a box containing a gold chain. They read the letter to the blind and feeble Galileo and presented him with the chain. He took the letter and the box into his hands, but returned the chain, feeling it was wrong to accept it.

However, Galileo's hopes for his method being adopted were ruined when all four of the appointed commissioners died within the next nine months, and after that, the government of Holland never resumed its interest in Galileo's method.

❧ DEATH·OF·A·GENIUS ❧

GALILEO'S LAST days were spent quietly at his villa in Arcetri. He had many visitors there, including the grand duke of Tuscany, Ferdinand II, and Galileo's friend from Siena, Archbishop Ascanio Piccolomini. In 1641 Galileo revisited the idea of adding pendulums to clocks in order to make them more accurate. Since he was blind, it was impossible for him to put the idea into motion, so he set his son Vincenzio in charge of constructing a working model.

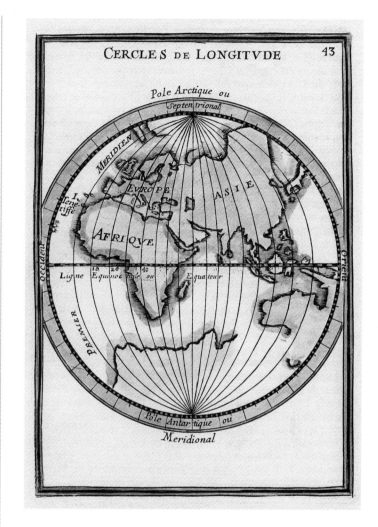

Seventeenth-century map of the world showing lines of longitude.

ALL THROUGH HIS CHILDHOOD, Galileo was exposed to music. His father, Vincenzo, was a cloth merchant who was known for his musical skills. Galileo quickly showed that he, too, had musical talent, but his father discouraged him from the profession. "You will see, as I have, that you cannot live by means of your musical skills alone," he told his son, and encouraged him instead to become a doctor. But science beckoned, and Galileo soon became a famous astronomer and mathematician. As it turned out, his fascination with music never died. Nearly 70 years after his first encounter with his father's music, Galileo wrote a scientific explanation of how sound waves work and how strings vibrate.

MATERIALS
* Thick rubber band
* A friend
* Guitar

Sound travels through the air in waves, which vibrate the eardrum and send a signal to the brain. Imagine sound waves as ripples in a pool of water. In the same amount of time, a high sound makes many more waves than a low sound. As part of his discussion about music and sound, Galileo identified the three ways to change the tone of a string.

1. **Tension of string:** Stretch a thick rubber band a little between your two thumbs, and have a friend pluck it. Stretch it more, and let your friend pluck it again. Stretch it a few more times. The more taut the rubber band becomes, the higher the note that is produced. Now, let the rubber band relax until there is no tension. When your friend plucks it, the note produced is so low you may not hear it unless you bring the rubber band close to your ears. The same applies to a guitar string. When you tighten a string, the sound produced is higher, and when you loosen a string, the sound is lower.

2. **Length of string:** Another property of music is that a shorter string will produce more rapid sound waves and higher notes than a longer string. Pluck a guitar string, then place your finger on each fret (ridge) and pluck, starting at the top of the guitar. You will notice the notes getting higher and higher as the length of string plucked

gets shorter. If you have ever looked inside a piano or seen a harp, you may have noticed the different string lengths. Galileo found that if you pluck a string, then pluck half its length, you will get the same note one octave (eight notes) higher. (Music relies heavily on octaves. The best representation of an octave is the popular "do re mi fa so la ti do.") Try this on a guitar.

3. **Thickness of string:** Since a guitar must have strings that are all the same length, each string is a different thickness or material to create different notes. Which string produces the higher note on a guitar—the thickest or thinnest string?

✤ JOHN MILTON

John Milton was born in England in 1608. A well-educated man, he largely taught himself by reading extensively. He enthusiastically read literature in English, Latin, Greek, and Italian. Milton wrote poetry, publishing "Lycidas" around 1638. That same year his father sent him on a year-long journey to the European continent, where he could further his education and experience of the world. It was on this journey that he was supposed to have met with Galileo at Galileo's residence in Arcetri.

Milton spent a great deal of his life as a political radical, publishing pamphlets in support of the execution of England's King Charles I. He was on the Puritan side during the English Civil War. He also published an essay defending freedom of the press. In 1660 the political movement he supported was crushed, and Milton was imprisoned. This period was called the Reformation. Friends intervened on his behalf, and he was released, but he suffered a heavy fine and the loss of much of his property.

In addition to defeat and poverty, by this time Milton had also gone blind, a special hardship for a writer and student of literature. With the help of assistants to whom he dictated, Milton accomplished the writing of three great poems of epic achievement. The first and greatest of these was *Paradise Lost* (1667), which tells the tale of Lucifer's (the Devil's) revolt against God as well as the fall of Adam and Eve in the Garden of Eden. In book one of *Paradise Lost*, Milton wrote:

> *Hung on his shoulders like the moon,*
> * whose orb*
> *Through optic glass the Tuscan artist views*
> *At evening, from the top of Fesole.*

The "Tuscan artist" he refers to is Galileo, who studied the skies with his telescope from a hill in a town called Fiesole, near Florence.

In another part of *Paradise Lost*, Milton ponders the question of the Copernican theory:

> *What if the sun*
> *Be center to the world; and other stars,*
> *By his attractive virtue and their own*
> *Incited, dance about him various rounds?*
> *Their wandering course, now high, now low,*
> * then hid,*
> *Progressive, retrograde, or standing still,*
> *In six thou seest; and what if seventh to these*
> *The planet earth, so steadfast though she seem,*
> *Insensibly three different motions move?*

Paradise Lost is considered one of the great masterpieces of English literature. Milton followed this with *Paradise Regained*, telling of Christ's temptation in the wilderness, and *Samson Agonistes*, a tragedy (both 1671).

Milton died in 1674 from complications of gout (inflammation of the joints). Despite people's dislike of his political views, his literary achievements were praised. His last works took on themes of both the Renaissance (war, love, religion, hell, heaven, the universe, classical references) and the Reformation (earnestness and individuality, Christianity, the core of man's conscience). These two contrasting influences in his life combined in his writings to produce one of the greatest epic poems of all time.

John Milton.

Though blind and ailing, Galileo retained his sarcastic playfulness through the end. In a letter to a man named Rinuccini in March 1641, he wrote:

> We, Catholics everywhere, should reject it [the Copernican theory]. The unimpeachable authority of the Holy Scriptures is contrary to this system, as the celebrated theologians have explained; their unanimous declaration proves to us that the earth, placed in the center, is immovable and that the sun revolves around it. The conjectures on which Copernicus and his partisans have pretended to establish the idea to the contrary falls before the well-founded argument of the all powerful divinity . . . If moreover the observations and experiences of Copernicus seem insufficient to me, those of Ptolemy, Aristotle, and their sectarians [followers] are even more erroneous and more deceiving; demonstrating the falsity of their system without surpassing the limits of human knowledge is easy.

Galileo invited his friend Benedetto Castelli's pupil, named Evangelista Torricelli (1608–1647), to stay with him after having been impressed by a manuscript penned by the young man. Torricelli arrived at Arcetri just a few months before Galileo's death.

Right up until the last days, Galileo tried to stay active. On December 20, 1641, just days before his death, he wrote to one of his daughter-in-law's family members, Alessandra Bocchineri Buonamici:

> I received your very friendly letter; it was to me a great consolation; I have found myself, for several weeks, in bed, gravely ill. I thank you as cordially as I can for the so very kindly interest you bring and for the mercy that you accomplish toward me in my misfortune and my miseries.
>
> For the moment I don't have need for linens; but I remain doubly obligated for the attention that you give to my needs. I beg of you, excuse the brevity of my letter. I suffer horribly, meanwhile I kiss your hand and also that of your spouse.

Galileo's close friend Vincenzo Viviani (1622–1703) was there with him toward the end, along with Torricelli and Galileo's old friend Castelli. On

Evangelista Torricelli.

January 8, 1642, at the age of nearly 78, Galileo died as the result of a two-month bout of fever and heart ailments. Viviani, Torricelli, Galileo's son, Vincenzio, his daughter-in-law, Sestilia Bocchineri, and the local priest were all there at his bedside when he breathed his last. In his will, Galileo left everything to his son. His surviving daughter, Arcangela, received only a small annual sum.

Galileo was originally to be buried at the Santa Croce Church in Florence with a great funeral. According to his wishes, he wanted to be buried in the ancient family sepulchre (vault) at the church. His body was sent from Arcetri to Santa Croce in preparation. A collection was taken up among friends and supporters who wished to erect a monument to Galileo. His enemies, however, tried to prevent this from happening.

On January 23, 1642, Pope Urban VIII formally objected to this idea; he did not think it was fitting because Galileo had caused a scandal for the Church. Word was sent to the grand duke of Tuscany that, because Galileo was under sentence of the Inquisition when he died, he could not be buried with pomp and circumstance. In the end, Galileo was laid to rest in an obscure corner of a small side chapel at Santa Croce. An epitaph (inscription) was finally placed there in 1656.

Galileo's pupil Viviani was the first to write down the story of Galileo's life and collect some of his letters in a volume called *Racconto istorico della vita di Signor Galileo Galilei, Nobile Fiorentino* (*Stories Told About the Life of*

(CHARTING THE CYCLOID CURVE)

AS A MATHEMATICIAN, Galileo was fascinated by the many unique mathematical relationships of geometric shapes. Galileo was very interested in a special shape: the curve (called a cycloid curve) that resulted when a point on a wheel was followed as the wheel was rolled in a complete revolution on a straight line.

MATERIALS

* Frisbee (flying disc)
* Highly adhesive tape (such as packing tape or good clear tape)
* 1-inch- (2.5-cm-) long piece of blue or black crayon
* Piece of 30-by-40-inch (75-by-100-cm) foam board
* A friend

Using the tape, attach the crayon to the edge of the Frisbee so it is perpendicular to the edge. Use several strips of tape back and forth across to secure the crayon fragment so the tip is just protruding from the edge of the Frisbee. Hold the foam board upright so the 40-inch (100-cm) length is on the ground. Hold the Frisbee on the floor and bring it up against the board, so that the crayon is on the bottom, outside (right) edge of the Frisbee and the crayon is touching the board. Now, have your friend slowly and steadily roll the Frisbee to the left until the crayon has gone a full revolution and is at the bottom of the Frisbee again, on the inside (left) edge.

Look at the outline of the shape you have traced on the board. Galileo thought that this shape had special properties and might be applied to practical uses, such as the arch of a bridge. He wanted to figure out what the relationship was between the circle and the shape that was traced by the moving point. One method he used to figure it out was to cut out the shape and weigh it in comparison to the weight of the circle. In this way, he discovered the area of the cycloid curve was about three times that of the circle that created it.

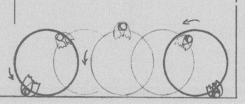

Signor Galileo Galilei, Noble Florentine), published in 1654, 12 years after Galileo's death. Though only a teenager when he met the ailing and blind Galileo, the Florence-born Viviani spent a great deal of time with Galileo. He considered himself a dear friend and heir to the legend of Galileo's greatness. Viviani later became the court mathematician to the grand duke of Tuscany, a position that Galileo had held.

Even later in his life, Viviani still fondly remembered Galileo. In 1693, nearly 50 years after his mentor's death, Viviani had a long passage praising Galileo engraved onto the front of his house, with a bronze bust of Galileo as the centerpiece over his door.

Permission to construct a more fitting resting place for the scientist was finally received in the 18th century, more than 30 years after Viviani's death. On March 12, 1737, with great ceremony, Galileo's remains were taken from

❁ RENÉ DESCARTES

The French philosopher, mathematician, and scientist René Descartes (1596–1650) was interested in astronomy. He was 30 years younger than Galileo, and represented the next generation of scientists. In fact, he was about to publish a work called *Le Monde* (*The World*) when word came out about Galileo's troubles with the Inquisition in 1633.

Descartes did not want to get into trouble as well, so he decided against publication of that work. "This has astonished me so much that I have almost determined to burn all my papers, or at least never to let them be seen by anyone,"

Descartes wrote when he heard about the Galileo affair. He wished to live in peace, without being persecuted for something he wrote.

He did, however, later go on to develop some of his ideas about planetary motion. He believed that each planet was surrounded by some sort of invisible matter. The solar system has the sun at its center, and the planets all revolve around the sun within its vortex (whirlpool) of invisible matter. Shown here is a 17th-century depiction of the "System of Descartes," or his view of how the solar system worked.

System of the planets, according to René Descartes. ➤

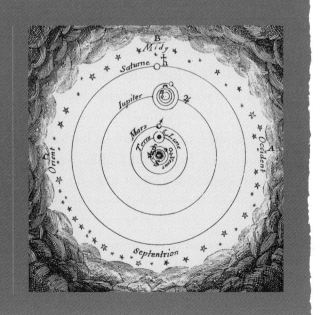

the chapel at Santa Croce and relocated to a proper mausoleum in the church of Santa Croce. Viviani's remains were also relocated and placed next to Galileo's. The monument there contains a bust of Galileo, along with figures representing astronomy and geometry.

The great English poet Lord Byron later wrote about Santa Croce and the famous men buried there in his poem "Childe Harold":

> *In Santa Croce's holy precincts lie*
> *Ashes which make it holier, dust which is*
> *Even in itself an immortality,*
> *Though there is nothing save the past, and this,*
> *The particle of those sublimities*
> *Which have relapsed to chaos: — here repose*
> *Angelo's, Alfieri's bones, and his*
> *The starry Galileo, with his woes;*
> *Here Machiavelli's earth returned to whence it rose.*

Galileo's son, Vincenzio, died in 1649, while working on the construction of the pendulum that his father had explained to him. After Galileo's death, Vincenzio lost enthusiasm for the pendulum clock, and only resumed work on it a month before his own death, hiring an ironsmith to make some of the parts. When he died, Vincenzio was in the midst of trying to solve some technical problems associated with making the pendulum work properly to keep time in a clock. Some years later, in 1658, a Dutch mathematician named Christiaan Huygens actually succeeded in building the first pendulum clock.

Despite the condemnation that befell Galileo, several of his descendants were also involved in the Catholic Church. Galileo's grandson Cosimo became a missionary. His great-grandson Carlo became a monk, while another great-grandson, Cosimo, became a parish priest at Santa Maria Novella di Chianti. In 1992 Pope John Paul II issued a formal statement declaring that the Church's conviction of Galileo was an error.

Wᴵᵀᴴ ᴼᴿ ᴡᴵᵀᴴᴼᵁᵀ the approval of the Catholic Church, science was on a path of no return. Copernicus, Brahe, Galileo, and Kepler had all helped start a revolution that led to the invention of many instruments used to study both the earth and the heavens. They had also aroused the curiosity of the scientific world.

New discoveries in the skies continued to be made. During the 1650s, Huygens discovered that what Galileo saw next to Saturn was not a moon but a ring. He also discovered an actual moon of Saturn. In 1687 Sir Isaac Newton published a work on how gravity allows the planets to orbit the sun. In 1705 Edmond Halley calculated the path of the comet that now bears his name and is visible on Earth every 76 years.

In 1675 King Charles II of England founded the Royal Observatory at Greenwich in an attempt to develop a system of longitude. Today, Greenwich is the prime meridian (0 degrees longitude) and is used to calculate standard time around the world. Astronomers, using increasingly powerful telescopes, discovered three more planets orbiting the sun in the far reaches of the solar

Portrait of Galileo on the Italian 2,000 lire note.

system. These telescopes were far stronger than anything Galileo had ever used. English scientist Sir William Herschel discovered the planet Uranus in 1781. U.-J.-J. Le Verrier of France discovered Neptune in 1846, and C. W. Tombaugh of the United States discovered the tiny and very distant Pluto in 1930.

By the 1950s the United States and Russia had developed space programs that involved the creation of rockets capable of being launched into space. The Russians were the first to send a human being into space in 1961, when Yuri Gagarin orbited the earth on a spacecraft named *Vostok I*. During the 1960s, orbiting spacecraft sent back photos of the moon.

After years of preparation and training, in 1969 the United States sent the Apollo 11 mission to the moon with three astronauts on board. On July 20 the lunar module landed on the moon, and Neil Armstrong and Buzz Aldrin became the first humans to set foot on the satellite that Galileo had studied in detail with his telescope nearly 400 years earlier. The astronauts spent 21 hours on the moon's surface and collected 46 pounds (21 kg) of moon rocks. Several more missions were sent to the moon over the next several years, before the lunar program was shut down.

Unmanned space exploration continued. In 1976 the *Viking 1* lander touched down on Mars, and for the first time we were able to see detailed color photographs of the planet's surface. Again in the 1990s and in 2004, spacecraft landed on Mars and sent back pictures. The Hubble Space Telescope (deployed into orbit in 1990) snapped beautiful photographs of never-before-seen objects located deep in space.

NASA launched the Galileo mission in 1989. An exploratory spacecraft named *Galileo* was sent into space aboard the space shuttle *Atlantis* to study Jupiter and her moons. *Galileo* arrived near the giant planet in 1995 and eventually traveled 2.8 billion miles (45 million km) and sent back about 14,000 pictures before ending its mission in 2003 upon crashing into Jupiter.

Galileo's greatest contributions to science were his unfailing curiosity and his quest for truth. He let observation be the logic that guided his arguments and showed the world how to think.

The Observatory at Greenwich, England, founded 1675.

RESOURCES

✤ POPES OF GALILEO'S TIME

NAME	NAME AT BIRTH	REIGN DATES	LIFE SPAN
Pius IV	Giovanni Angelo de' Medici	1559–65	1499–1565
Pius V	Antonio Ghislieri	1566–72	1504–1572
Gregory XIII	Ugo Buoncompagni	1572–85	1502–1585
Sixtus V	Felice Peretti	1585–90	1520–1590
Urban VII	Giambattista Castagna	1590	1521–1590
Gregory XIV	Niccolò Sfondrati	1590–91	1535–1591
Innocent IX	Giovanni Antonio Facchinetti	1591	1519–1591
Clement VIII	Ippolito Aldobrandini	1592–1605	1536–1605
Paul V	Camillo Borghese	1605–21	1552–1621
Gregory XV	Alessandro Ludovisi	1621–23	1554–1623
Urban VIII	Maffeo Barberini	1623–44	1568–1644

✤ THE GRAND DUKES OF TUSCANY DURING GALILEO'S TIME

NAME	LIFE SPAN
Cosimo I de' Medici	1519–1574
Francesco I de' Medici	1541–1587
Ferdinand I de' Medici	1549–1609
Cosimo II de' Medici	1590–1621
Ferdinand II de' Medici	1610–1670

Pope Gregory XIII, who had the calendar reformed in 1582.

❈ GLOSSARY OF KEY TERMS

abjuration: renunciation of a statement or writing

acceleration: increasing speed

admonition: serious warning

arc: a curved line that is any fragment of a circle

astronomy: scientific study of the stars, planets, and space

axis: an invisible line through the center of a celestial sphere around which it rotates or spins

blasphemy: speaking or writing against God or the Bible

catapult: a weapon used to hurl large objects

celestial: heavenly; in the sky

circumference: the total length around a circle or sphere

comet: traveling celestial body composed of ice, rock, and dust

conjecture: an educated guess

constellation: man-made map in the sky that includes several stars and makes a "picture" of an animal or mythical person

Copernican theory: theory that the earth and planets revolve around the sun, and that the earth also rotates on its axis, causing day and night

decree: an official order

density: *see* specific gravity

diameter: the width of a sphere or circle

displacement: when an object is placed into liquid and causes some of the liquid to overflow or be displaced

doctrine: a way of thinking

Dominican: a member of an Order of the Catholic Church

eclipse: when one celestial body passes in front of another, obscuring its view

ellipse: a closed curve that is a perfect oval

ethics: the study of morals and civil behavior

fortification: a structure with thick walls built for defense against attack

Franciscan: a member of an order of the Catholic Church

gravity: the force that pulls down on all objects within the earth's atmosphere

heresy: speaking, writing, or acting against the Catholic Church, a crime punishable by torture and death in Galileo's time

heretic: person found guilty of heresy

hydrostatic balance: invention of Galileo's that figured an object's weight using water

hypothesis: a supposition or assumption, based on scientific observation

illegitimate: not born of a marriage

Inquisition: a group within the Catholic Church that was created specifically to deal with heretics

irrigation: man-made method for watering crops

Jesuits: an order of the Catholic Church

latitude: system of imaginary lines on the globe that go east and west, telling you how far north or south you are located

logic: the study of scientific reasoning

longitude: system of imaginary lines on the globe that go north and south, telling you how far east or west you are located

mass: weight

matter: anything that takes up space and has mass

mechanics: the study of energy and forces on objects

Middle Ages: time before the Renaissance when advances in science had slowed

nebulae: cloudy regions in the heavens that are often remains of exploded stars

optics: the study of lenses and the mechanics of the eye

orbit: the motion of any heavenly body around another

parallax: difference in the apparent location of a distant object seen from two different points

patron: one who provides money and sponsors works of art, science, or literature in return for name recognition

penance: an act of devotion to show you are sorry for having sinned

pendulum: a weight on a string, wire, or cable that can swing freely

permutation: a mathematical combination, used in reference to the different possible results in gambling

philosophy: the pursuit of wisdom

physics: the science of motion and physical properties of objects

pious (piety): religiously devoted and observant

plague: contagious disease that killed millions between the 14th and 17th centuries

probability: mathematical odds that an event will occur

Protestant Reformation: a movement begun by Martin Luther, during which millions of people broke away from the Catholic Church

Ptolemaic system: theory that all the planets and the sun revolve around the earth

pulsilogia: an instrument that uses a pendulum to measure the pulse rate

quarantine: an isolated place for people (or sometimes whole cities) who have contagious and deadly diseases

recant: take back something you write or say

Renaissance: rebirth of science and art that occurred during the 15th and 16th centuries in Europe

satellite: orbiting body, such as a moon

sector: instrument used to measure angles and perform calculations

sextant: instrument used to measure the altitude of heavenly bodies

solar system: a star and the planets that revolve around it—in our case, the sun and the Earth, Mars, Mercury, Venus, etc.

specific gravity: density of an object

sunspot: a dark spot on the surface of the sun that is caused by a disturbance on the sun

supernova: a star that has exploded

telescope: instrument Galileo invented to enlarge distant objects

theology: study of religion

treatise: a comprehensive writing on a particular subject

velocity: speed

volume: the amount of space something takes up

✸ GLOSSARY OF KEY PEOPLE

Apian, Peter and Philip father and son astronomers of the 16th century who scientifically observed comets. Philip was the teacher of Michael Maestlin.

Archimedes Ancient Greek mathematician whose ideas on floating bodies Galileo contradicted

Aristotle Ancient Greek philosopher, some of whose scientific ideas were disputed by Galileo

Bellarmino, Cardinal Roberto priest who gave Galileo a warning in 1616 not to teach or hold the Copernican theory

Caccini, Tommaso priest who spoke out against Galileo in 1614, starting a sequence of events that led to the trial of Galileo 19 years later

Capra, Baldassar a former pupil of Galileo's who tried to claim credit for one of Galileo's inventions

Castelli, Benedetto friend of Galileo's for many years

Cesi, Federico friend of Galileo's and founder of the Lincei Academy, of which Galileo was a member

Copernicus, Nicolaus monk and scientist who in 1543 proposed that the earth revolves around the sun

Cosimo II Galileo's patron, Ferdinand I's successor

da Vinci, Leonardo an Italian artist and scientist of the 16th century

del Monte, Marquis Guidobaldo an early patron of Galileo

Ferdinand I Galileo's first patron, a member of the Medici family

Ferdinand II Cosimo II's successor, who was unable to save Galileo from the Inquisition

Foscarini, Father Paolo Antonio mathematician whose book that defended the Copernican theory was banned by the Catholic Church

Galilei, Arcangela Galileo's younger daughter, a nun at a convent along with her sister

Galilei, Maria Celeste Galileo's older daughter, who wrote him many letters from the convent where she was a nun

Galilei, Vincenzio Galileo's only son

Galilei, Vincenzo Galileo's father

Grassi, Horatio a Jesuit astronomer who wrote about comets

Grienberger, Father Christopher mathematician and contemporary of Galileo's

Hipparchus an early Greek astronomer who studied the motion of the sun and moon

Kepler, Johannes German mathematician and astronomer who was friendly with Galileo

Luther, Martin founder of the Protestant movement in the early 16th century

Maestlin, Michael astronomer and teacher of Kepler

Medici family powerful Florentine family whose members included popes, queens, and other notable people, including Galileo's patrons

Niccolini, Francesco Galileo's friend, the Tuscan ambassador at Rome, who talked to the pope on Galileo's behalf several times

Piccolomini, Ascanio Galileo's friend, the Archbishop of Siena

Pope Paul V pope when Galileo was warned against teaching the Copernican theory

Pope Urban VIII pope who had been Galileo's friend, but who turned against Galileo when his *Dialogue of the Two Chief Systems* was published in 1632

Ptolemy, Claudius ancient astronomer and mathematician whose theory was that the sun and planets orbited the earth

Pythagoras ancient Greek mathematician

Riccardi, Niccolo papal censor who delayed publication of *Dialogue of the Two Chief Systems* for many months

Sagredo, Giovanni Francesco Galileo's close Venetian friend

Scheiner, Christoph one of Galileo's enemies, beginning with a disagreement on the sunspots

Torricelli, Evangelista young scientist who spent time with Galileo at the end of Galileo's life

Viviani, Vincenzo pupil of Galileo's, who spent time with him toward the end of Galileo's life

❈ GLOSSARY OF KEY PLACES IN ITALY

Arcetri: location of the villa where Galileo spent his last days (1633–42)

Bellosguardo: home near Florence where Galileo lived for some time beginning in 1617

Florence: city where Galileo's family moved when he was a child

Padua: city where Galileo taught for 18 years

Pisa: city where Galileo was born

Rome: headquarters of the Catholic Church, location where Galileo's trial was held

Siena: city where Galileo spent the first five months of his confinement in 1633

Tuscany: region of Italy where Pisa and Florence are located

Venice: canal-filled city near Padua where Galileo brought his newly invented telescope

❋ GALILEO'S KEY WRITINGS

The Assayer treatise on comets and the nature of light

Floating Bodies an early work on the properties of materials in water

On Sunspots relates Galileo's discoveries about the sunspots

Starry Messenger publication in which Galileo wrote of his discoveries made with the telescope

Two Chief Systems book in which Galileo discusses the Ptolemaic system and Copernican theory

Two New Sciences book in which Galileo discusses projectile motion and material strength

❋ WEB SITES

The Galileo Project of Rice University

http://es.rice.edu/ES/humsoc/Galileo/

This Web site has a great deal of information about all aspects of Galileo's life.

The Galileo Legacy Site

http://galileo.jpl.nasa.gov/

This Web site tells of the Galileo space mission, which discovered many new details about Jupiter and its moons.

Galileo's Battle for the Heavens

http://www.pbs.org/wgbh/nova/galileo/

This is the Web site for a public television program that was part of the NOVA series. The site has information on Galileo's life and experiments.

Institute and Museum of the History of Science

http://brunelleschi.imss.fi.it/catalogo/

If you click on "Exhibition Areas" and then "Room IV-Galileo Galilei," you can take a virtual tour of some of the museum's Galileo-related objects and instruments.

Catholic Encyclopedia

http://www.newadvent.org/cathen

This is an excellent Catholic encyclopedia that supplies more information about all the popes, as well as key figures such as Galileo and Copernicus.

❋ PLANETARIUMS AND ASTRONOMY/SPACE MUSEUMS

ARIZONA

Pima Air & Space Museum

6000 East Valencia Road

Tucson, Arizona 85706

(520) 574-0462

http://www.pimaair.org/

CALIFORNIA

Gladwin Planetarium

Santa Barbara Museum of Natural History

2559 Puesta del Sol Road

Santa Barbara, California 93105

(805) 682-4711, Ext. 405

http://www.sbnature.org/events/gladwin.php

Griffith Observatory
2800 East Observatory Road
Los Angeles, California 90027
(323) 664-1181
http://www.griffithobs.org/Generalinfo.html

Morrison Planetarium
California Academy of Sciences
875 Howard Street
San Francisco, California 94103
(415) 321-8000
http://www.calacademy.org/planetarium/

Palomar College Planetarium
Earth Sciences Department
1140 West Mission Road
San Marcos, California 92069
(760) 744-1150, Ext. 2512
http://www.palomar.edu/astronomy/
    planetarium/school_shows.htm

UCLA Planetarium and Telescope Shows
Division of Astronomy and Astrophysics
University of California, Los Angeles
520 Portola Plaza, 8th floor
Los Angeles, California 90095
(310) 825-4434
http://www.astro.ucla.edu/planetarium/

COLORADO

Fiske Planetarium
Campus Box 408
University of Colorado
Boulder, Colorado 80309
(303) 492-5002 or (303) 492-5001
http://www.colorado.edu/fiske/home.html

DISTRICT OF COLUMBIA

The National Air and Space Museum
Flagship Building on the National Mall
Independence Ave at 4th Street, SW
Washington, D.C. 20560
(202) 633-1000
http://www.nasm.si.edu/museum/flagship.cfm

FLORIDA

**Astronaut Memorial Planetarium
and Observatory**
1519 Clearlake Road
Cocoa, Florida 32922
(321) 433-7373
http://www.brevardcc.edu/planet/

Calusa Nature Center and Planetarium
3450 Ortiz Avenue
Fort Myers, Florida 33905
(239) 275-3435
http://www.calusanature.com/
Information.htm

ILLINOIS

Adler Planetarium & Astronomy Museum
1300 South Lake Shore Drive
Chicago, Illinois 60605-2403
(312) 922-STAR
http://www.adlerplanetarium.org/

Museum of Science and Industry
57th Street and Lake Shore Drive
Chicago, Illinois 60637
(773) 684-1414
http://www.msichicago.org/index.html

KANSAS

Kansas Cosmosphere and Space Center
1100 North Plum
Hutchinson, Kansas 67501
(620) 662-2305 or (800) 397-0330
http://www.cosmo.org/

MASSACHUSETTS

Center for Space Physics
Boston University
725 Commonwealth Avenue, Room 506
Boston, Massachusetts 02215
(617) 353-5990
http://www.bu.edu/csp/csp_history.html

Charles Hayden Planetarium

Museum of Science

Science Park

Boston, Massachusetts 02114

(617) 589-0100

http://www.mos.org/doc/1114

MISSISSIPPI

Rainwater Observatory and Planetarium

1 Fine Place

French Camp, Mississippi 39745

(662) 547-6377

http://www.rainwaterobservatory.org/info/
info.html

NEW YORK

Intrepid Sea-Air-Space Museum

Pier 86, 12th Avenue & 46th Street

New York, New York 10036

(212) 245-0072

http://www.intrepidmuseum.org/

Rose Center for Earth and Space

American Museum of Natural History

Central Park West at 79th Street

New York, New York 10024

(212) 769-5100

http://www.amnh.org/rose/haydenplanetarium
.html

PENNSYLVANIA

Fels Planetarium

222 North 20th Street

Philadelphia, Pennsylvania 19103

(215) 448-1200

http://sln.fi.edu/tfi/info/fels.html

TENNESSEE

Bays Mountain Planetarium

853 Bays Mountain Park Road

Kingsport, Tennessee 37660

(423) 229-9447

http://www.baysmountain.com/planetdept/
astronomy.html

TEXAS

Houston Museum of Natural Science

1 Hermann Circle Drive

Houston, Texas 77030

(713) 639-4629

http://www.hmns.org/museum_info/museum
_info.asp

Space Center Houston

1601 NASA Parkway

(formerly NASA Road 1)

Houston, Texas 77058

(281) 244-2100

http://www.spacecenter.org/about.html

UTAH

Clark Planetarium

110 South 400 West

Salt Lake City, Utah 84101

(801) 456-STAR

http://www.clarkplanetarium.org/

VIRGINIA

Steven F. Udvar-Hazy Center

National Air and Space Museum

14390 Air and Space Museum Parkway

Chantilly, Virginia 20151

(202) 357-2700

http://www.nasm.si.edu/museum/udvarhazy/

❋ SELECTED BIBLIOGRAPHY

Baker, Robert H. *Astronomy*. 1930. Reprint, Princeton, N.J.: D. Van Nostrand Company, 1959.

Brecht, Bertolt. *Leben des Galilei (The Life of Galileo)*. Translated by Desmond I. Vesey. 1943. Reprint, London: Eyre Methuen, 1974.

Brewster, Sir David. *The Martyrs of Science*. 1841. Reprint, London: Chatto and Windus Publishers, 1874.

Burnham, Robert, ed. *Star and Sky (Discovery Travel Adventures)*. New York: Langenscheidt Publishers, 2000.

Chasles, Philarète. *Galileo Galilei, sa vie, son procès et ses contemporains*. Paris: Poulet-Malassis, 1862.

Davis, Kenneth C. *Don't Know Much About the Universe*. New York: HarperCollins Publishers, 2001.

Drake, Stillman, and C. D. O'Malley, trans. *The Controversy on the Comets of 1618: Galileo Galilei, Horatio Grassi, Mario Guiducci, Johann Kepler*. Philadelphia: University of Pennsylvania Press, 1960.

Galilei, Galileo. "Concerning the Two New Sciences." In *Great Books of the Western World*, edited by Robert Maynard Hutchins, vol. 28. Chicago: Encyclopaedia Britannica, 1952.

———. *Opere di Galileo Galilei*. Milan: Societa Tipografica de Classici Italiani, 1811.

Gebler, Karl von. *Galileo Galilei and the Roman Curia*. London: C. Kegan Paul & Co., 1879.

Hoskin, Michael, ed. *The Cambridge Illustrated History of Astronomy*. Cambridge, Eng.: Cambridge University Press, 1997.

Levitt, I. M. and Roy K. Marshall. *Star Maps for Beginners*. 1942. Reprint, New York: Fireside Books, 1980.

Mattison, Hiram. *A High School Astronomy: In Which the Descriptive, Physical, and Practical are Combined, with Special Reference to the Wants of Academies and Seminaries of Learning*. 1853. Reprint, New York: Mason Brothers, 1859.

Methuen, Charlotte. *Kepler's Tübingen: Stimulus to a Theological Mathematics*. Aldershot, Eng.: Ashgate Publishing Company, 1998.

Moore, Patrick. *Sun, Myths and Men*. 1954. Reprint, New York: W. W. Norton and Company, 1968.

The Private Life of Galileo. London: Macmillan and Co., 1870.

Ranke, Leopold von. *The Popes of Rome: Their Church and State in the Sixteenth and Seventeenth Centuries*. Glasgow: Blackie and Son, 1846–47.

Ridpath, Ian. *The Concise Handbook of Astronomy*. New York: Gallery Books, 1986.

Sagan, Carl. *Cosmos*. New York: Random House, 1980.

Sobel, Dava. *Galileo's Daughter*. New York: Walker and Company, 1999.

———. *Longitude*. New York: Walker and Company, 1995.

The Story of Galileo, the Astronomer of Pisa. London: T. Nelson and Sons, 1889.

Viviani, Vincenzo. *Racconto historico della vita di Signor Galileo Galilei, Nobile Fiorentino*. 1654. Reprint, Venice: Tipografia di Alvisopoli, 1826.

Whitfield, Peter. *The Mapping of the Heavens*. London: British Library, 1995.

INDEX

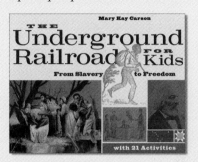

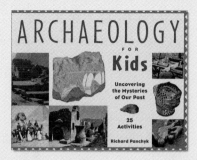

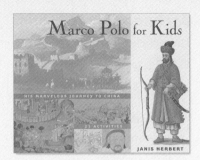